From Our Kitchen to Yours!

Recipes to intrigue, entertain and satisfy!

Established 1867

Published by

GENERAL STORE
PUBLISHING HOUSE

499 O'Brien Rd., Box 415, Renfrew, Ontario, Canada K7V 4A6
Telephone (613) 432-7697 or 1-800-465-6072
www.gsph.com

ISBN 1-897113-27-7
Printed and bound in Canada

Cover design, formatting and printing by
Custom Printers of Renfrew Ltd.

Food Editors: Debbie Clouthier, Richard Gorman, Jane Karchmar,
Shirley Plant and Eric Vivian

Library and Archives Canada Cataloguing in Publication

From our kitchen to yours : recipes from Lapointe Fish
restaurant / food editors, Richard Gorman ... [et al.].

ISBN 1-897113-27-7

1. Cookery (Fish)   I. Gorman, Richard (Richard B.)

TX747.F76 2006   641.6'92   C2006-903108-8

Welcome to

LAPOINTE
FISH LIMITED

Lapointe Fish Limited takes pride in presenting this, our latest cookbook, to customers and the general public. For over a century, we have maintained the highest standards for freshness, quality, and service. Our business is fresh fish and seafood, and we treasure the continuing loyalty and satisfaction of our clientele.

Behind this cookbook stand the talented chefs of Lapointe's restaurants. Consumers these days look for both enjoyment and nutrition in their dietary choices, and seafood scores high on both counts. Here you will find a selection of recipes for each of the fish species usually stocked in our retail stores.

In addition to great recipes, this cookbook includes information on buying, storage, preparation, and nutrition. Reading the preliminary sections will repay your time investment many times over. Selling fish is a business, but cooking and savouring the "fruits of the sea" is an art. We hope you'll enjoy the seafood experience from shopping in our stores, to cooking and barbecuing, to sharing your creations with family and friends around the table. Bon appétit!

The Vivian Family
Owners and Operators for three generations

The
LAPOINTE
STORY

In the summer of 1867, Canadian Confederation became a reality, and the city of Ottawa, although little more than a lumber settlement, became the new capital of the Dominion of Canada. In the spring of the same year, Moise Lapointe, "widely and most favourably known," [*Ottawa Journal*] had established his freshwater fish and seafood business and became the third such merchant in the city. Through steadfast quality control—a remarkable feat without the benefit of refrigeration—Mr. Lapointe built a solid reputation.

Photo of Lapointe's shop front, 1867.

Although there were times that the sale of ice was more profitable than that of fish, it is recorded that Moise Lapointe soon netted more than three-quarters of the city's retail fish trade. So well did the Lapointe name become established in just a few years that several other merchants set up seafood businesses under the name Lapointe, but their ventures ultimately failed.

The City of Ottawa Directory, 1870–71, carried this advertisement: "Moise Lapointe — Dealer in all kinds of Fresh and Pickled Fish, Fresh Salmon, Oysters, Lobsters…Wholesale and Retail." The directory's 1874–75 edition reads: "Game and Fish Dealer— Purveyor to His Excellency the Governor General."

Lapointe's in the By Ward Market, Ottawa, 1883.

The business was first located in the old Lower Town Market building. When that structure was destroyed by fire in 1883, the store was moved to the then new By Ward Market building. Twenty-five years ago, the firm was moved to its present location in the By Ward Market by Eric Vivian Jr., who took over from his father in 1972.

Since the early years, many other competitors have come and gone, but by remaining true to the original standards established by Moise Lapointe, the firm has maintained its status as Ottawa's headquarters for fresh fish and seafood.

The
NUTRITIONAL
VALUE OF FISH

Statement of Dr. Frederick J. Stare, Professor of Nutrition, Harvard University,
to the U.S. Senate Select Committee on Nutrition and Human Needs

Fish is an excellent food nutritionally. In fact, it is hard for me to think of any single food that is nutritionally superior to fish, and few that are as good. Some time ago, I stated that in the year 2000, Americans will be consuming more fish. That was said recently when one of our local radio announcers came around for an interview on what Bostonians would be eating and drinking in the year 2000, part of a one-hour documentary on how things would be in that year. In addition, I mentioned that Bostonians and other Americans would be consuming less butter but drinking more milk, eating more food but with less calories, and will be drinking fluoridated water, and starvation and malnutrition will be unpleasant memories of a generation ago.

Why did I mention fish first? Because more fish belongs in diets designed to lessen the development of our main cause of death today—coronary heart disease.

Over 500,000 people in the United States die each year from heart attacks—one-third of them men in the prime of life. Certain habits or conditions, called risk factors, increase the chances of a heart attack. Among these risk factors is a high level of cholesterol and frequently other fatty substances in the blood.

There is substantial evidence that dietary changes can alter the level of these fatty substances in the blood and help prevent heart attacks. The most important dietary changes are fewer total calories, less saturated fat in the diet, less cholesterol in the diet, and more poly-unsaturated fats. Fish, except shellfish, is a positive contribution on all of these points.

The exception for shellfish is really more of an academic point than one of practical implications. Shellfish are reasonably rich sources of cholesterol—containing two to three times the amount contained in meat or in other fish—but still only half the amount in eggs.

For most Americans, shellfish are not consumed with great frequency in the diet as are eggs, hence our usual recommendation to the public for diets designed to lower the level of cholesterol in the blood, and we do not advise the restriction of shellfish.

We would all be in better health if we consumed fish more frequently, at least four to six times per week. More people would learn to like fish if it were properly prepared, if techniques or gadgets were devised to cook fish without smelling up the kitchen and house, and especially if one would learn to enjoy fish during childhood . . .

Reprinted from the Fisheries Council of Canada Bulletin

Seafood
NUTRITIONAL
CHART*

HF - High Fat Fish   **LW** - Low Fat Fish   **F** - Farm Raised
MF - Medium Fat   **na** - Not Available   **W** - Wild Caught

Note: These figures are to be used as rough guides only. Values vary with species, water temperatures, catch locations, season caught, etc.

SALTWATER FISH

200 grams 7 oz. Raw, edible portion	W - F	HF MF LF	Calories	Protein (grams)	Fat (grams)	Sodium (milligrams)	Cholesterol (milligrams)	Omega-3 (grams)
Bass/Chilean	W	HF	428	32.4	32.2	na	na	na
Bass/Striped, Red	W	LF	192	36.8	2.8	124	na	1.2
Bluefish	W	MF	248	40.0	8.4	120	118	2.4
Cod, Atlantic	W	LF	164	35.6	1.4	108	86	0.3
Cod, Pacific	W	LF	164	35.8	1.2	140	80	0.2
Flounder	W	LF	180	36.2	2.8	112	100	0.2
Grouper	W	LF	174	38.6	1.0	160	100	0.6
Haddock	W	LF	160	36.6	1.0	120	120	0.2
Halibut	W	LF	210	40.0	2.4	118	100	0.8
Herring	W	HF	300	36.6	17	150	160	3.4
Mackerel,Atlantic	W	HF	400	43.8	14.6	160	80	5.0
Mahi-mahi	W	LF	204	42.0	2.0	260	170	0.2
Monkfish	W	LF	140	31.0	2.0	36	70	na
Orange Roughy	W	LF	130	29.4	0.6	126	118	0.2
Pompano	W	HF	328	37.0	19.6	130	100	1.2
Salmon, Atlantic	F	MF	284	39.6	12.6	88	110	1.6
Salmon, Chinook	W	HF	360	40.0	20.8	90	132	2.8
Salmon, Coho/Sliver	W	MF	292	40.0	11.2	92	78	1.6
Salmon, Sockeye	W	MF	332	42.6	17.2	94	124	2.4
Shark	W	LF	180	40.0	2.0	156	96	na
Skate	W	LF	190	40.0	2.0	180	na	na
Snapper, Red	W	LF	200	41.0	2.6	128	74	0.7
Sole	W	LF	140	29.8	1.0	110	90	0.2
Swordfish	W	MF	240	38.8	8.8	140	100	0.4
Tuna, Albacore	W	MF	204	36.4	6.0	100	50	2.6
Tuna, canned, water packed	W	LF	260	59.2	1.0	712	40	0.2
Tuna, Yellow fin	W	MF	216	46.8	20.0	74	90	2.8

Seafood
NUTRITIONAL
CHART*

HF - High Fat Fish   **LW** - Low Fat Fish   **F** - Farm Raised
MF - Medium Fat   **na** - Not Available   **W** - Wild Caught

Note: These figures are to be used as rough guides only. Values vary with species, water temperatures, catch locations, season caught, etc.

FRESHWATER FISH

200 grams 7 oz. Raw, edible portion	W - F	HF MF LF	Calories	Protein (grams)	Fat (grams)	Sodium (milligrams)	Cholesterol (milligrams)	Omega-3 (grams)
Bass, Striped	F	LF	228	37.8	7.2	140	138	0.6
Catfish	F	MF	232	36.4	8.6	126	96	0.6
Char, Arctic	F	HF	326	22.8	15.8	130	54	1.0
Smelt	W	MF	194	35.2	4.8	120	140	1.4
Sturgeon	F	MF	210	32.2	8.0	568	na	0.6
Tilapia	F	LF	196	37.0	4.8	104	na	0.6
Trout, Rainbow	F	HF	390	23.0	22.8	102	100	3.0
Whitefish	W	HF	324	37.6	18.0	114	96	1.0

CRUSTACEANS

Crab, Alaskan King	W	LF	150	30.4	1.6	140	120	0.6
Crab, Blue	W	LF	174	36.0	2.2	583	156	0.6
Crab, Dungeness	W	LF	162	34.6	2.6	532	118	0.6
Lobster	W	LF	180	33.8	3.4	410	170	0.4
Shrimp	W	LF	180	37.6	1.6	240	316	0.6

MOLLUSKS

Abalone	F	LF	210	34.2	1.6	602	170	trace
Clams	F	LF	160	22.0	3.0	160	80	0.2
Mussels	F	LF	150	24.4	3.2	160	50	1.0
Octopus	W	LF	152	30.0	3.0	na	244	0.4
Oysters	F	LF	162	19.0	4.6	212	100	1.4
Scallops	W	LF	164	30.3	0.4	320	100	0.4
Squid	W	LF	170	32.8	1.8	320	460	0.8

* Compiled from U.S.D.A. statistics

Buying, Preserving, and Dressing
FRESH FISH
AND SEAFOOD

Fish can be separated into four types: saltwater, shellfish, freshwater, and smoked fish. Saltwater fish can be further divided into white or oily fish. In white ocean fish, such as cod and halibut, the natural oils are found in the liver. The flesh of these types of fish is very delicate and easily digested. In oily fish—mackerel and herring, for example—the oils are distributed throughout the fish. These fish are extremely nutritious.

Fresh fish has a distinctive odour rather than an objectionable smell. Characteristically, fresh whole fish have clear, bright eyes, red gills, and tight, shiny scales covered with a natural slime. The flesh should feel firm and not separate from the bone easily. Live lobster and crab are rigid and lively rather than looking limp. Live oysters have tightly closed shells. When two oysters are tapped together, they will produce a sharp crack, not a hollow sound. Live clams also have tightly closed shells. The shell of a mussel might be open, but if the mussel is still alive, its shell will close tightly when pressed together.

When buying whole fish, allow one pound per serving. For dressed fish (entrails, head, and tail removed) or steaks, allow one-half pound per serving. Allow one pound of fish fillets for every three adults.

Preservation

Always have whole fish cleaned at the store. At home, wash the fish under running cold water, pat dry with paper towelling, wrap in waxed paper, and store in a cold area of the refrigerator. Use as soon as possible. Fresh fillets and steaks should be wiped with a damp cloth, wrapped, and refrigerated. Smoked fish should be wrapped, kept cold, and used as soon as possible for best flavor. Smoked salmon should be carefully wrapped in a clinging plastic wrap such as Saran Wrap®, since contact with the air will quickly dry very thin slices. The Fisheries Research Board of Canada (Bulletin #100, 1954) has proven that fresh fish can be kept up to twelve days (at 31.5°F/-0.3°C) without spoilage, providing proper sanitary conditions are observed.

Live lobster and crab should be packed in seaweed and then refrigerated. Do not place them in tap water. Oysters, clams, and mussels should be kept in a glass dish or paper bag in the refrigerator. Use as soon as possible. They should not be washed or shucked until needed for cooking or serving. Do not freeze in the shell. Shrimp should be kept frozen. If they are thawed, rinse them under cold water, wrap in wax paper, and refrigerate. Do not freeze shrimp that appears to be fresh as it has most likely been thawed. Refreezing causes a distinct loss of flavor. Frozen fish should be kept at 0°F/-18°C or lower and used immediately after thawing.

Skinning

Using a sharp knife, remove the fins and slit the skin down the backbone. Sprinkle the skin with salt to prevent your fingers from slipping. Lift the skin carefully away from the flesh at the tail, hold the knife at an angle to the skin, and, using a sawing motion with the knife, gently pull the skin away from the flesh.

Filleting

Remove the scales from the fish. Starting at the head, cut the fish down the center along the backbone. Cut the flesh away from the bone using a sweeping stroke and keeping very close to the bone.

English–Metric
CONVERSIONS
TABLES

Dry & Liquid Measure

millilitres (ml) = number of ounces (oz) x 30*

number of litres (L) = number of quarts (qt) x 0.95

1000 ml = 1 L

50 ml = 1/4 cup (c)

75 ml = 1/3 c

125 ml = 1/2 c

175 ml = 3/4 c

250 ml = 1 c

1 L = 4 c

Small Measure

1 ml = 1/4 tsp

2 ml = 1/2 tsp

5 ml = 1 tsp

15 ml = 1 Tbsp

30 ml = 2 Tbsp

45 ml = 3 Tbsp

Use this conversion to obtain the approximate size of baking pan needed for a metric recipe.

Seafood
TEXTURE/FLAVOUR
COMPARISON

Factors affecting the flavor of seafood include harvest location, water salinity and quality, season of the year, and other local conditions.

Texture	Light Flavour	Moderate Flavour	Piquant Flavour
Delicate	Flounder Pollock Sole	Butterfish	Oysters
Moderate	Haddock Ocean Perch Orange Roughy Salmon (Atlantic) Salmon (Chum) Scallops Snapper Tilapia Trout Walleye Whitefish	Mullet Salmon (Coho) Smelts	Salmon (Sockeye)
Firm	Catfish Cod Crab Grouper Halibut Mahi Mahi Sea Bass Shark Shrimp Sturgeon Whiting	Clams Lobster Monkfish Pompano Tuna	Mackerel Mussels Swordfish

Basic
COOKING
INSTRUCTIONS

Bear in mind that fish is naturally tender, juicy, and flavourful—overcooking destroys taste, texture, and tenderness. When cooked, fish should be served immediately.

Baking
You can bake any species or cut of fish—fillets, steaks, whole dressed fish. Season fish with salt, pepper, and other herbs and spices as desired. Place fish on a well-buttered shallow pan and bake in a preheated oven at 400°F/200°C. Allow ten minutes per inch of thickness of fresh fish, and twenty minutes per inch if frozen. Whole fish may be stuffed. Baste the fish from time to time with white wine or melted butter. Small whole fish are often baked *"en papillote"* by wrapping the entire fish in buttered, heavy waxed paper or foil (no need to baste).

Boiling
Boiling is a good way of cooking not only large whole fish such as salmon or haddock but also steaks from very large fish such as tuna or swordfish. Wrap fish in cheesecloth and tie securely. Place fish in water seasoned with lemon juice, salt, and herbs to taste. Fish can also be cooked in Court Bouillon (see index). Bring liquid to a boil, reduce heat, and simmer gently by keeping the liquid temperature below 190°F/88°C. Allow ten minutes of cooking time per inch of thickness. Drain and serve.

Broiling
Fish cut into steaks (three-quarters to one inch thick) and small fish such as herring are best for broiling. Preheat the broiler. Dip steaks in milk and dust lightly with flour, or brush fish with melted butter, and season as desired. Place the fish two inches below the heat source for steaks and four to five inches for whole fish. Baste with butter occasionally. Turn once. Cooking time depends on the thickness, with steaks usually requiring about five minutes each side.

Deep Frying
Fish should be coated with beaten eggs and breadcrumbs or batter before frying. Coating protects the fish from the intense heat of the fat. Fillets and shellfish fry well. Place one layer of fish in a frying basket and fry in fat

preheated to 375°F/190°C until golden brown, about five minutes. The remaining fat can be used for other foods, since the coating is sealed as soon as it touches the hot fat.

Pan Frying

When cooking small fish such as smelts, fry the entire fish. Cut larger fish into steaks or suitable portions. Dip fish in milk and roll in flour, breadcrumbs, or oatmeal. Carefully lay the fish in a pan of hot butter or fat (not smoking), using about one-quarter inch of fat in the pan. Fry over medium heat until lightly browned, about four minutes. Turn fish and brown for three minutes.

Poaching

This method is good for cooking large whole fish such as salmon. Wrap the fish in foil or cheesecloth. Fill a roasting pan or fish poacher with Court Bouillon (see index). Lay the fish in the pan, cover, and place in a preheated 400°F/200°C oven or on the stove-top over medium heat. Simmer and ensure that the liquid does not boil. Cook ten minutes per inch of thickness. Lift fish out of liquid, unwrap, garnish, and serve.

Sautéing

Use a white-fleshed fish or fillets such as cod, haddock, or whitefish. Fillets may be used whole or cut into portions. Melt butter in a pan, add chopped parsley, milled black pepper, lemon juice, and chopped chives or shallots. Place fish in pan and cook over medium heat. When half cooked, add white wine and allow the liquid to reduce to about half the original volume. Cover and simmer until cooked.

Steaming

Steaming helps make fish even more digestible, particularly recommended when cooking for people on fairly bland diets. Wrap fish in cheesecloth and tie. Fill a large pot with two inches of water and add salt and the juice of half a lemon. Cover and bring to a boil. Place fish on a wire rack or tray in pot so that it does not touch the water. Cover and steam about ten minutes per inch of thickness.

LOBSTER

Lobsters are saltwater crustaceans; never immerse them in tap water. Store them in the refrigerator until needed, and cook them as soon as possible. The lobster marketed in the Ottawa region *(Homarus Americanus)* is a distant relative of shrimp and crayfish.

The Fisheries Research Board of Canada reports that about two-thirds of Canada's estimated lobster catch of fifty million pounds is shipped live to distant markets—mainly the United States, Great Britain, and Europe. Lobster is available all year round, but vary considerably in price. From May 15 to June 30 and from October 15 to November 30, the lobster supply is greatest and lower prices generally prevail. Many people prefer to buy hen lobster because of the spawn that is often made into lobster butter and used in sauces. Others believe that the meat of the cock lobster is finer and firmer in texture.

Lobster may be purchased live, cooked, or as canned lobster meat. Lobster tails are also available frozen and ready to cook. When purchased live, lobster should show movement of the legs, and the tail should curl under the body. Reject weak or droopy-looking specimens. Lobsters should be alive until cooking. To check a cooked lobster for freshness, arch back the curled tail and release; the fresher the lobster, the firmer the spring-back. Discard a cooked lobster with a drooping tail. Lobster on the market vary from chicks weighing about one-half pound each to jumbos weighing two to two-and-a-half pounds. Allow one pound of unshelled lobster per serving.

If you need fresh, uncooked lobster meat, place the live lobster on its back, cover tail with a cloth and hold firmly with your free hand. Using a sharp knife, quickly cut through the head at the small indentation that can be seen about halfway along the head. (The lobster dies immediately.)

Cooking Instructions

Fill a container with enough water to cover the lobsters. For each quart of water, add coarse salt to taste; sea salt if desired. You can add seasonings and fresh lemon juice to the water for extra flavour. When the water has been brought to the boil, plunge the lobster in headfirst and cover the container. When the water returns to boiling, reduce heat and simmer 15 to 20 minutes. Serve your steaming lobster with lemon and drawn butter, or cold with mayonnaise. If you intend to eat the lobster cold, cooking it in Court Bouillon (see index) is recommended. Cool quickly under running water and drain.

How to Shell a Lobster

Twist off the claws.

Crack each claw with a hammer, nutcracker, or similar instrument.

Separate the tail from the body by arching back the tail until it cracks.

Break off the flippers at the end of the tail. Push tail meat out using a fork inserted where the flippers were attached. Remove the dark vein running through the body.

Remove the small claws from the body. They also contain meat that can be drawn out by sucking as through a straw.

Turn lobster onto its belly and, using a sharp heavy knife, split the body in two, leaving the outer shell intact.

In the head area there is a small plastic-like sac that should be discarded. In the body cavity you will find the tomalley or liver (green when cooked) and the coral or spawn–both are tasty and make good eating. Adding a lemon butter sauce or other preferred flavouring is suggested.

Your lobster feed will be more enjoyable if you give your guests lobster bibs and invite them to eat the lobster with their hands. A simple green salad or corn on the cob will complete the meal.

OYSTERS

Oysters have been called the most valuable seafood for humans; they are delicious when served raw on the half-shell or cooked. The quality of an oyster depends more upon the area in which it was grown than upon any other single factor. Almost everyone has heard of the famous Malpeque Bay oysters. Actually, the name Malpeque is now used popularly to denote all oysters harvested around Prince Edward Island. There are other oysters available in Canada, notably Caraquet oysters from New Brunswick and oysters harvested in Cape Breton and Nova Scotia.

An average East Coast oyster may produce as many as half a billion eggs in a season. Of these, only about 430 reach adult size. Oyster harvesting in the temperate zones takes place in autumn and winter. The old saying that oysters should only be eaten in a month containing the letter R does indeed have some basis in fact, as they are generally the tastiest and plumpest at that time. However, due to modern farming technology as well as dramatically improved marketing techniques and air transportation, the oyster season has been extended to the point that varieties of oysters are available on a year-round basis.

Oysters are sold in the shell or shucked. Shucked oysters are used for soups, chowders, and the like. In Canada, the federal government controls oyster grading. Grading is not by size but by shape. According to regulations, the length of "choice" grade oysters must not exceed one-and-a-half times the greatest width. The length of "standard" grade oysters must not exceed one-and-three-quarters times the greatest width. These two grades are most widely sold in this country. Fancy and commercial grades are also available.

Oysters contain 86.9 percent water, 6.2 percent protein, and 6.9 percent carbohydrates, fats, and ash. There is about the same amount of nourishment in a quart of oysters as in three-quarters of a pound of lean beef or a quart of milk.

Oysters remain alive until the shucking knife cuts the meat away from the shell. Therefore, handling oysters is a critical problem; they must be stored at a temperature between 35° and 40°F (2° and 4°C), which induces hibernation and slows down their metabolism. Oysters survive best in a climate of high humidity. This is why Canadian oysters are not washed until consumed.

Preparation of Shell Oysters

Wash oyster under running cold water, scrub well with a brush, and drain. Do not let oysters stand in the water.

Holding the broad side of the oyster in the palm of the hand, insert a strong knife (use one with a hand-guard attached or wear heavy gloves) between the shells, twist, and pry apart the shells. Cut the oyster meat from the shell. The meat is now ready for cooking, or it can be served as is.

Serve raw oysters on the half-shell with lemon juice, white wine, tabasco sauce, vinegar, or seafood sauce. Shucked oysters should be eaten as soon as possible after opening.

SHRIMP

Shrimp is marketed in this area in a variety of forms, all of them frozen: cleaned and cooked, cleaned and ready to cook, raw in the shell, cooked in the shell, and as frozen shrimp meat. One pound of unshelled shrimp will yield about half a pound of cooked, peeled, and deveined shrimp, enough to serve three or four persons. Despite the extra labour involved in preparing unshelled shrimp, many people consider them a better buy because less shrinkage occurs during the cooking process and the initial cost per pound is lower. Since a raw, peeled, deveined shrimp is unprotected by its shell, it can shrink by as much 25 percent when cooked.

Shrimp consumed in North America come from the waters of Canada, the United States, Mexico, South America, and India. Some shrimp producers claim that the northern shrimp known as *pandalus borealis* is more flavourful than the shrimp caught in waters farther south. However, the northern shrimp is smaller and can have a count of up to one hundred per pound.

New on the market in recent years are the Matane shrimp caught in Canadian waters between Sept Iles and Ste Anne des Monts and also in the Bay of Fundy. These shrimp are sold cooked, peeled, and deveined as shrimp meat and as cooked, frozen, and unshelled. The Matane variety has been successful chiefly because of rigid quality control procedures. All operations are carried out by hand, and the shrimp are processed on land within hours of being caught.

Although larger warm-water shrimp may be more bland tasting than cold-water varieties, they can be perked up considerably by marinating the cooked, cleaned shrimp in a mixture of one part lemon juice to one-and-a-quarter parts cold water to which a dash of salt, chopped fresh parsley, and ground pepper has been added. Use a non-metallic dish. Cover and chill for about an hour.

Shrimp are graded according to the number per pound. A count of 10–15 to 21–25 per pound is usually referred to as jumbo size, although larger sizes are available up to 4–6 count; 31–35 to 41–50 are classified as "medium"; 51–60 to 70 and more are classified as "small."

Cooking Instructions

Boiling is the basic method. Bring salted water to a boil. Add shrimp. When water returns to a boil, reduce heat and simmer. Cook "small" shrimp 1–2 minutes, "medium" 2–3 minutes, and "jumbo" 3–5 minutes. Shrimp can be sautéed in a frying pan by turning quickly on high heat for a few minutes.

How to Peel and Devein Shrimp

Shrimp may be cleaned before or after cooking. Starting on the underside of the shrimp, use your fingers or a paring knife to peel off the shell. Remove the sand vein running along the back. Rinse. Less shrinkage occurs if shrimp are cooked unshelled.

SAUCES

Aioli

This is a rich mayonnaise made with thick, green olive oil, heavily flavoured with garlic. Try when eating steamed clams or mussels.

2 egg yolks
1 tsp/5 ml Dijon mustard
4 garlic cloves, minced

2/3 cup/150 ml olive oil
juice of 1/2 lemon
dash salt

Place the egg yolks in a bowl with the mustard and garlic. While whisking, add the olive oil in a steady stream until a thick emulsion is formed. Add the lemon juice, season with salt, and let it stand for an hour before serving.

Basic Fish Stock

Fish stock carries flavour. It is not a sauce on its own, so don't expect it to taste delicious. The best bones to use are halibut, monkfish, and flounder bones. Avoid salmon, trout, and sea bass, as they can make the stock chalky.

2 lb/1 kg cleaned fish bones
1 leek, chopped
1/2 onion, chopped
2 carrots, chopped

1 celery stalk, chopped
1 fennel bulb, chopped
few sprigs of thyme
1 cup/250 ml white wine

Sweat the vegetables and herbs in a little olive oil until softened. Break up the bones into chunks, so they fit in the pan, and give it a good stir. Add the wine and enough water to cover. Gently simmer for 40 minutes, skimming any froth from the top with a spoon. Strain and then return to the pan and boil to reduce by a third. This is the process where water will evaporate and intensify the flavour. Just keep it gently boiling until a third of it is gone.

Basic Tartar Sauce

1 1/2 cups/375 ml mayonnaise
1 dill pickle, chopped fine
4 shallots, chopped fine
2 anchovies, chopped fine
1 Tbsp/15 ml each of capers,
    parsley, tarragon and chervil,
    chopped

heavy cream
1 tsp/5ml dry mustard
1/2 tsp/2ml each of lemon juice
    and sugar
salt and pepper to taste

In a bowl mix mayonnaise, dill pickle, shallots, anchovies, capers, parsley, tarragon, chervil and dry mustard. Thin the sauce with heavy cream until preferred consistency obtained, and season with lemon, sugar, salt, and pepper. Serve with any fried fish or shellfish.

Caper Sauce

1/4 cup/50 ml butter
1/4 cup/50 ml flour
2 cups/500 ml strained fish cooking liquid from steamed or poached fish
6 Tbsp/90 ml capers with juice

Make a roux with butter and flour, and add enough liquid, stirring as you add it, to give the consistency of a white sauce. Stir in capers.

Cucumber Sauce

2 large cucumbers
1 small onion
2 celery stalks with leaves

1/2 cup/125 ml light chicken or
    fish stock
1 Tbsp/15 ml lemon juice

Peel cucumbers and onion; wash celery and trim; chop all three into small pieces. Add to the stock and lemon juice in a heavy saucepan and simmer until cucumbers are translucent and soft enough to be mashed with a spoon. Purée everything in a blender or push through a food mill.

Dill Sauce

1/2 cup/125 ml watercress leaves
1/4 cup/50 ml scallions, sliced
1/4 cup/50 ml fresh dill, chopped
1 garlic clove, minced
2 anchovy fillets, chopped

1 cup/250 ml mayonnaise
2 Tbsp/30 ml lemon juice
2 Tbsp/30 ml olive oil
1/2 cup/125 ml sour cream
1/2 tsp/2 ml salt
1/4 tsp/1 ml black pepper

In a blender combine all ingredients except sour cream, until creamy. Remove from blender; taste for seasoning and adjust if needed. Add sour cream and mix well. Chill before serving.

Egg Sauce

2 Tbsp/30 ml butter or margarine
2 Tbsp/30 ml flour
1 cup/250 ml milk
1/4 cup/50 ml cream
1 Tbsp/15 ml lemon juice

2 hard-boiled eggs, chopped
2 Tbsp/30 ml pimento, diced (optional)
1/2 tsp/2 ml salt
dash of pepper

Melt butter or margarine in small saucepan over low heat. Blend in flour, salt, and pepper. Stir in milk and cream; cook, stirring constantly, until thick and smooth. Fold in lemon juice, eggs, and pimento.

Garlic Butter

8 garlic cloves
2 handfuls fresh parsley, finely chopped
handful of tarragon, chopped

2 cups/500 ml unsalted butter, softened
pinch salt

Place all the ingredients except the butter into a food processor and blend to a smooth paste. In a bowl mix the paste thoroughly and evenly with a wooden spoon into the butter. Roll in plastic wrap and store in freezer.

Homemade Mayonnaise

2 egg yolks
1 tsp/5 ml Dijon mustard
1 tsp/5 ml white wine vinegar
1/3 cup/75 ml vegetable oil

1/3 cup/75 ml olive oil
juice of 1/2 lemon
salt and pepper to taste

Place the egg yolks in a bowl with the mustard and vinegar. Mix the oils together and pour onto the egg yolks in a steady stream whilst whisking until you have a thick, creamy mayonnaise. Lastly, season and add the lemon juice.

Lime Marinade

zest of half a lime
2 limes, juiced
2 Tbsp/30 ml fresh coriander leaves, chopped
2 tsp/10 ml olive oil
salt and pepper to taste

Combine the ingredients in a mixing bowl. Cover and refrigerate for a few hours. This is an ideal preparation for grilling or broiling.

Court Bouillon

6 cups/200 ml cold water
1/2 cup/100 ml chopped onions
1/2 cup/100 ml chopped celery
1/4 cup/50 ml chopped leeks,
   tender white part only,
   washed thoroughly

1/4 cup/50 ml chopped carrots
1 bouquet garni (parsley, thyme,
   bay leaf) or just toss the herbs
   in with the vegetables

Combine the above ingredients in a stockpot over medium heat. Bring to a boil, reduce the heat, and let simmer gently, uncovered, until the vegetables are tender, about 20 minutes. Add 3 tablespoons/30 ml lemon juice or white wine vinegar.
Simmer for another 10 minutes. Strain into a clean pot or heatproof plastic container.
Season with salt and ground black pepper to taste.

Mango Citrus
Sauce for Fish

flesh of one ripe mango, cubed
juice and zest of half a lime
2 Tbsp/30 ml orange or citrus marmalade
2 Tbsp/30 ml corn starch
2 Tbsp/30 ml water
2–3 Tbsp/30–45 ml sherry, dry or medium

Toss the mango pieces into a medium saucepan with the lime juice
and zest and the marmalade. Heat gently to bubbling while mashing
with a potato masher. When the sauce starts to bubble, reduce heat,
cover, and simmer 5 minutes. Mix the water and cornstarch and,
while stirring the sauce constantly, add cornstarch mixture by
teaspoons (5-mls) until the sauce thickens as desired. Stir in the
sherry and pour over cooked fish. This recipe makes enough to
cover four average-size fillets.

Rosemary and Anchovy Butter

1/2 tin of anchovy fillets (50 g)
2 garlic cloves
2 sprigs of rosemary (pick the leaves off and discard the branch)
2 cups/500 ml unsalted butter

Put the anchovies with their oil into a food processor with the garlic
and rosemary. Blend until smooth and stir into the softened butter.
Roll in plastic wrap and store in freezer.

Salmon Barbecue Sauce

1 cup/250 ml brown sugar
1/2 cup/125 ml honey
1 tsp/5 ml chipotle pepper sauce
1/2 cup/125 ml cider vinegar
1 small can of tomato sauce
salt and pepper to taste

Combine the ingredients in a saucepan and simmer 5–10 minutes. A great sauce for grilling salmon or trout.

Sauce Béchamel (White Sauce)

1/4 cup/50 ml butter
1/4 cup/50 ml flour
2 cups/500 ml of room-temperature milk
salt and pepper to taste

Melt butter in a saucepan. The instant it is melted, remove pan from heat and sprinkle in flour, spoon by spoon; stir while adding and continue to stir until well blended. Slowly add milk, stirring constantly. The sauce will become smooth and faintly yellow. Return the pan to the heat and stir some more. As sauce starts to bubble, add just a touch of salt and pepper. Continue cooking over low heat until sauce thickens.

Sauce Hollandaise

4 egg yolks
1 Tbsp/15 ml light cream
1 Tbsp/15 ml tarragon vinegar or lemon juice
1/2 cup/125 ml butter
cayenne pepper
salt

In a double boiler over low heat, beat egg yolks with light cream and tarragon vinegar or lemon juice. Continue beating the eggs with a whisk until they begin to thicken. Add butter, bit by bit, and continue beating the sauce until it is thick. Should the mixture curdle, immediately beat in 1 or 2 tbsp/15 or 30 ml of boiling water in order to rebind the emulsion. Add lemon juice, and salt and cayenne to taste. Serve with any hot or cold poached fish.

Summery Green Basil Pesto

This dish can be stored in the fridge, in a sealed jar with a layer of olive oil on top. It is delicious stirred into pasta or used as a dressing for roasted vegetables.

1 large bunch green basil, stalks removed
1 garlic clove
1 Tbsp/15 ml pine nuts
2 Tbsp/30 ml parmesan cheese
1/3 cup/75 ml olive oil
salt

Put all the ingredients into a food processor and pulse until you have a coarse, creamy paste. Add salt to taste.

Tomato Mango Salsa

1 tomato
1 mango
1 small onion
1 lime, juiced
1/4 cup/50 ml fresh coriander leaves, chopped
salt and pepper to taste

Dice the tomato, mango, and onion. Place in a small saucepan with the lime juice and salt and pepper. Simmer for 5 minutes. Remove from heat, stir in coriander, and chill thoroughly before serving.

White Wine Sauce

1 Tbsp/15 ml shallots, chopped
1 Tbsp/15 ml parsley stems, chopped
1 2/3 cups/400 ml white wine
5 tsp/25 ml butter

2 Tbsp/30 ml flour
2/3 cup/150 ml fish stock or fish poaching liquid
1/2 cup/125 ml heavy cream
salt and pepper to taste

Simmer the shallots and parsley stems in 2/3 cup/150 ml wine until reduced by half to a flavourful infusion. Meanwhile, melt the butter over low heat, stir in the flour to make a smooth, pale roux, and add the fish stock or strained poaching liquid and remaining 1 cup/250 ml wine. Cook over low heat, stirring often, until the sauce is very smooth and thick, and somewhat reduced. Strain the infusion into it, mix well, then add the cream. Continue to simmer, without allowing the sauce to boil, until it is reduced and blended to your taste. Season with salt and pepper if you like.

SOUPS,
CHOWDERS,
AND
MEDLEYS

A Classic Spanish
Swordfish Stew

2 lb /1 kg fresh swordfish steak, skinned and cut into bite-size pieces
1/4 cup/50 ml olive oil
3 shallots, chopped
2 garlic cloves, chopped
8 oz/225 g can tomatoes, chopped
1 Tbsp/15 ml tomato paste
2 lb/1 kg potatoes, sliced
1 1/2 cup/375 ml vegetable stock
2 Tbsp/30 ml lemon juice
1 red bell pepper, seeded and chopped
1 orange bell pepper, seeded and chopped
20 black olives, pitted and halved
salt and pepper
crusty bread, to serve

Garnish:
fresh flat-leaf parsley sprigs

Heat the oil in a pan over low heat, add the shallots, and cook, stirring
frequently, for 4 minutes, or until softened. Add the garlic, tomatoes,
and tomato paste, cover, and let simmer gently for 20 minutes.

Place the potatoes in an ovenproof pot with the stock and lemon
juice. Bring to a boil, then reduce the heat and add the bell peppers.
Cover and cook for 15 minutes.

Add the olives, swordfish, and the tomato mixture to the potatoes.
Season to taste with salt and pepper. Stir well, then cover and let
simmer for 7–10 minutes, or until the swordfish is cooked to your taste.

Garnish with parsley sprigs and lemon slices and serve with crusty
bread.

Serves 4.

Devilled Eggs
with Shrimp Medley

1/2 cup/125 ml cooked fresh shrimp, chopped
2 Tbsp/30 ml fresh lemon or lime juice
8 large eggs
1/4 tsp/1 ml dry mustard
3 Tbsp/45 ml mayonnaise
1/2 tsp/2 ml cider vinegar
2 Tbsp/30 ml horseradish
salt and pepper to taste
fresh chives or parsley, chopped

Place the shrimp in a glass bowl, and toss with the lemon juice. Set aside. Place the eggs in a medium saucepan, cover with water, and bring to a boil. Let boil for about 30 seconds, remove from the heat, and let sit for 15 minutes. Run the eggs under cold water, peel, and halve.

Place the cooked yolks in a bowl, and mash with the mustard, mayonnaise, cider vinegar, and horseradish, salt, and pepper to taste. Drain the shrimp, and mix them with the egg yolks. You may need to add additional mayonnaise. Stuff the whites, garnish with chopped chives or parsley leaves. Refrigerate before serving.

Serves 3 to 4.

*No good fish goes anywhere
without a porpoise.*

—Lewis Carroll

Fresh Crabmeat, Avocado and Mango Salad

1 lb/455 g fresh crabmeat, picked over for shells and cartilage
2 small avocados
2-3 Tbsp/30 to 45 ml combined lemon and lime juices
2 ripe mangoes
1/2 cantaloupe
4 lemon slices

Peel the avocados and dice into 1/2 inch pieces. Place in a large bowl, and toss with 2 Tbsp/30 ml of the citrus juice. Peel the mangoes and dice them into 1/2 inch pieces over the bowl. Save the mango juices that will drip into the bowl. Thoroughly toss with the crabmeat. Taste and season with additional citrus juice if needed.

Peel the cantaloupe and slice it into 12 pieces. Arrange the cantaloupe pieces and lemon slices on a large platter. Mound the crabmeat mixture in the centre of the platter. Chill for about 30 minutes before serving.

Serves 4.

Haddock and Lobster Chowder

5 medium potatoes, peeled and diced
2 medium onions, sliced
2 cups/500ml water
2 lb/1kg fresh haddock
2 lb/1kg cooked lobster
4 oz/115g butter
1 large can evaporated milk
salt and pepper to taste

Peel and dice the potatoes. Place in 2-quart/2 L size pan with water. Add the onion and cook 20 minutes.

Add the haddock, lobster, and butter. Simmer for 30 minutes.

Add evaporated milk. Simmer until chowder is hot (do not bring to a boil).

Serve with bread or pita.

Serves 6.

Harvey's Oyster Stew

18-24 shucked oysters with juice
1/4 cup/50 ml butter
1/4 cup/50 ml red onions, diced
2 Tbsp/30 ml flour
1/2 cup/125 ml dry white wine
1/4 cup/50 ml chicken stock
1 cup/250 ml heavy cream
1/4 tsp/1 ml black pepper
1/4 tsp/1 ml salt
1/4 tsp/1 ml paprika

Melt butter in heavy bottom saucepan. Sauté onion until transparent.
Add oysters (shucked) with their liquid and heat through, about 2 or
3 minutes. Melt remaining butter in a second heavy bottom
saucepan. Stir in flour to make a paste. Add seasoning (pepper, salt,
paprika). Gradually stir in wine, chicken stock, and cream over low
heat to avoid curdling.

Add shucked oysters with their juice and cook about five minutes,
stirring constantly.

Serves 2.

*We're definite in Nova Scotia—'bout things like
ships...and fish, the best in the world.*

– Canadian screenwriter John Rhodes Sturdy

Hearty Mussel Soup

2 lb/1kg cultivated mussels
8 cups/2L water
3 Tbsp/45ml olive oil
4 oz/115g butter
4 slices bacon, chopped
2 onions, chopped
2 garlic cloves, crushed
1/2 cup/125ml all-purpose flour

2 lb/1kg potatoes, thinly sliced
11/2 cups/375ml heavy cream
2 Tbsp/30ml lemon juice
2 egg yolks
salt and pepper to taste
2 Tbsp/30ml finely chopped
fresh parsley
lemon wedges

Rinse the mussels and discard any that do not close immediately when squeezed together.

Bring a large pan of water to a boil and add the mussels, oil, and a little pepper, and cook until the mussels open.

Drain the mussels, reserving the cooking liquid. Discard any mussels that are closed. Remove the mussels from their shells.

Melt the butter in a large saucepan and cook the bacon, onion, and garlic for 4 minutes. Carefully stir in the flour and then 5 cups/1.25L of the reserved cooking liquid.

Add the potatoes to the pan and simmer for 5 minutes. Add the above sauce and simmer for a further 10 minutes.

Add the cream and lemon juice, season to taste, and then add the mussels to the pan. Blend the egg yolks with 1–2 Tbsp/15–30ml of the remaining cooking liquid, stir into the pan, and cook for 4 minutes.

Ladle the soup into warm soup bowls, garnish with chopped fresh parsley and lemon wedges, and serve.

Serves 4

Market Seafood Soup

1/4 cup/50ml olive oil
2 large onions, finely chopped
3 garlic cloves, crushed
1 small red chili, finely chopped
1 tsp/5ml finely grated fresh ginger
3 Tbsp/45ml crunchy peanut butter
1 lb 12oz/800g canned chopped tomatoes
1 tin (14 oz/400ml) coconut cream
14 fl.oz/400ml canned coconut milk
2 pinches of ground cloves
4 Tbsp/60ml chopped coriander (cilantro) leaves
2 lb/1kg halibut, cut into large chunks
1 lb/455g medium shrimp, peeled and deveined
4 Tbsp/60ml chopped cashew nuts

Heat the oil in a deep saucepan and cook the onion gently for 5 minutes. Add the garlic, chili, and ginger and cook for 2 minutes. Stir in the peanut butter, tomatoes, coconut cream, coconut milk, ground cloves, and half of the coriander. Bring the mixture to a boil and simmer gently for 10 minutes.

Remove from the heat, allow to cool, and then blend in a food processor or blender until thick and smooth.

Return the sauce to the pan over medium heat. Add the halibut and cook for approximately 3 minutes, then add the shrimp and simmer until all the seafood is cooked--the shrimp will be pink and the fish opaque. Serve with the cashews and remaining coriander sprinkled over the top.

Serves 4

New England Clam Chowder

3 lb/1350 g littleneck clams
4 lean bacon slices, chopped
2 Tbsp/30 ml butter
1 onion, chopped
1 Tbsp/15 ml fresh thyme,
    chopped
1 large potato, diced

1 1/4 cups/300 ml milk
1 bay leaf
2/3 cup/150 ml heavy cream
1 Tbsp/15 ml fresh parsley,
    chopped
salt and pepper

Scrub the clams and put in a large pan with a splash of water. Cook over high heat for 3–4 minutes until all the clams have opened. Discard any that remain closed. Drain the clams, reserving the cooking liquid. Set aside until cool enough to handle.

Set aside 8 clams in their shells to garnish. Remove the remaining clams from their shells, coarsely chop if large, and set aside.

Heat a clean, dry pan over medium–high heat, add the bacon, and cook, stirring frequently, for 5 minutes, or until browned and crisp. Remove with a slotted spoon and drain on paper towels. Melt the butter in the pan, add the onion, and cook, stirring frequently, for 4–5 minutes until softened but not browned. Add the thyme and cook briefly before adding the potato, reserved clam cooking liquid, milk, and bay leaf. Bring to a boil, then reduce the heat and let simmer for 10 minutes, or until the potato is tender but not falling apart.

Let the soup cool slightly, then transfer to a blender or food processor and process until smooth.

Return the soup to the pan and add the shelled clams, bacon, and cream. Let simmer for an additional 2–3 minutes. Season to taste with salt and pepper and stir in the parsley. Ladle into warmed serving bowls, garnish with the reserved clams in their shells, and serve.

Serves 4.

Oyster Cream Soup

2 pints/1L fresh shelled oysters
1/4 lb/115g butter
6 shallots, minced
1 1/2 cups/375ml white wine
3 cups/750ml cream
2 tsp/10ml salt
1/2 tsp/2ml pepper
2 pinches paprika

Drain oysters.

Heat butter in a large saucepan and add oysters. Cook the oysters gently until they begin swelling and the small outer ring begins to curl, approximately 3 minutes.

Remove oysters from the butter with a slotted spoon and keep warm.

Add the shallots and wine to the butter left in the saucepan. Reduce the liquid to 1 cup/250ml by boiling at high temperature.

Heat the cream in a double boiler and add to the wine, stirring constantly. Add salt and pepper to taste. Add the oysters. Cook at low heat for 2 to 3 minutes.

Sprinkle with paprika and serve.

Serves 4

Scallop Soup

1 lb/455 g large fresh sea scallops cut into small chunks
4 cups/1 L rich chicken broth
1 egg white, beaten
2 slices ham, cut into strips
1 tsp/5 ml fresh coriander, finely chopped
salt

Heat chicken broth and keep at low simmer. Sauté scallops for a few minutes. Remove from heat and add the scallops to the chicken broth with a little salt to taste. Before serving stir in the beaten egg white and turn off heat immediately after adding. Stir well, pour into serving bowls, and garnish with ham strips and coriander leaves.

Serves 4.

*Do not tell fish stories where the people know you;
but particularly, don't tell them where
they know the fish.*

—Mark Twain

Tangy Crab & Citrus Salsa Medley

1/2 lb/225 g canned or fresh crabmeat, drained if canned and
thawed if frozen, flaked
1 red bell pepper, seeded and chopped
4 medium tomatoes, chopped
3 scallions, chopped
1 Tbsp/15 ml fresh flat-leaf parsley, chopped, plus extra sprigs to
garnish
1 fresh red chili, seeded and chopped
3 Tbsp/45 ml lime juice
3 Tbsp/45 ml orange juice
salt and pepper
lime wedges, to garnish

To serve:
thin carrot sticks
thin celery sticks
tortilla chips

Put the crabmeat, bell pepper, tomatoes, scallions, parsley, and chili
in a large, nonmetallic bowl. Add the lime juice and orange juice,
season to taste with salt and pepper, and mix well. Cover and let
chill in the refrigerator for 30 minutes to allow the flavours to
combine.

Remove the salsa from the refrigerator. Garnish with parsley sprigs
and lime wedges and serve with carrot and celery sticks and tortilla
chips for dipping.

Serves 2.

MAIN COURSES

Arctic Char Suprême

2 lb/1 kg fresh arctic char or
  salmon fillets
3 unpeeled pears, cut into
  eighths
1/4 cup/50 ml fresh orange juice
2 Tbsp/30 ml grapeseed oil
8 shallots, sliced
2 Tbsp/30 ml Grand Marnier
  liqueur
2 tsp/10 ml fresh chives,
  chopped

2 – 3 tsp/10 to 15 ml fresh
  ginger, minced
1 cup/250 ml bread crumbs
2 Tbsp/30 ml curry powder
3 Tbsp/45 ml flour
3 Tbsp/45 ml melted butter
3 Tbsp/45 ml toasted pecans,
  chopped
salt and pepper

Toss the pears with the orange juice in a large bowl and set aside.
Heat the oil and sauté the shallots over medium-low heat for 20 to
30 minutes, until softened and slightly caramelized. Drain the pear
slices and gently toss with the Grand Marnier, chives, ginger, and salt
and pepper to taste. Fan out attractively on a serving platter, and top
with the shallots.

Preheat the oven to 375°F – 400°F/190°C – 200°C.

Combine the breadcrumbs with the curry powder. Dip the arctic
char into the flour, shake to remove any excess, and place the fillets
into a baking dish. Pat the bread crumbs onto their surfaces, and
drizzle with the melted butter. Pour 2 tablespoons of water around
the fillets. Bake for about 12 minutes, or until the char is cooked
through and the bread crumbs are browned.

Arrange the char over the pears and sprinkle with the pecans.

Serves 4.

Herb and Garlic Striped Bass

2 lb/1 kg fresh striped bass fillet
2 Tbsp/30 ml olive oil
juice of 1 lemon
3 to 4 Tbsp/45 to 60 ml butter
1 Tbsp/15 ml garlic, minced
2 Tbsp/30 ml fresh sweet marjoram or parsley, chopped
1/2 tsp/2 ml orange zest

Preheat the oven to 375°F – 400°F/190°C – 200°C. Marinate the fish
in the oil and lemon juice for about 30 minutes in a large bowl in
the refrigerator. Either grill the fish or bake it for approximately 10
minutes, turning once. The amount of time depends upon the
thickness of the fillet.

Meanwhile, heat the butter in a saucepan and sauté the garlic for
about 3 minutes, stirring frequently. Do not brown. Add the sweet
marjoram and orange zest, if using. Remove the pan from the heat.

Pour garlic and herb butter over the fish just before serving.

Serves 4.

Calamari/Squid Cakes

2 cups/500 ml fresh cleaned squid
2 cups/500 ml fresh bread crumbs
1/4 cup/50 ml freshly grated parmesan cheese
4 garlic cloves, minced
1/4 cup/50 ml fresh parsley, finely chopped
1 egg
1/4 cup/50 ml olive oil
salt and pepper

Place squid in a food processor and pulse 6 times, until finely chopped. Transfer to a large bowl, then add bread crumbs, parmesan cheese, garlic, 3 Tbsp/45 ml parsley, egg, and season to taste with salt and pepper. Mix together well.

Wet hands to prevent calamari mixture from sticking, then form mixture into 3″ cakes. Heat oil in a large skillet over medium-high heat. Fry cakes until browned, about 3 minutes per side. Drain on paper towels and serve garnished with remaining parsley.

Serves 4.

Calamari/Squid in Plum Sauce

1 1/2 lb/680 g cleaned fresh squid tubes
3 Tbsp/45 ml flour
2 eggs, lightly beaten
3 cups/750 ml breadcrumbs
oil, for deep-frying

Chili plum sauce
1 tsp/5 ml oil
1 garlic clove, minced
1 cup/250 ml dark plum jam
1/3 cup/75 ml white vinegar
1–2 tbsp/15–30 ml bottled chopped chili or sweet chili sauce

Dry the squid tubes/calamari with a paper towel. Cut the calamari into rings by cutting vertically through squid tube.

Season the flour well and use to coat the calamari rings. Then dip in the beaten egg, drain off the excess, and toss in the breadcrumbs, patting them lightly onto the rings and shaking off the excess. Refrigerate for 10 minutes. Heat the oil in a large heavy-based pan to 350°F/180°C.

Fry the calamari in batches until crisp and golden, and drain well. Use a slotted spoon to remove the crumbs from the oil and between batches.

To make the sauce, heat the oil in a small pan. Add the garlic and cook until it is just starting to colour. Add the jam, vinegar, and chili. Stir over medium heat until well blended. Thin with a little warm water if necessary. Serve with the calamari rings.

Serves 4.

Calamari/Squid Neapolitan

2 lb/1 kg fresh cleaned calamari/squid
1 garlic clove, minced
3 Tbsp/45 ml butter
2 cups/500 ml canned diced tomatoes
12 black olives, pitted and chopped
1 Tbsp/15 ml raisins
1 Tbsp/15 ml pine nuts, chopped
1/2 cup/125 ml water
toast slices
salt and pepper to taste

Cut squids into small pieces, and wash well. Brown the garlic in the
butter in a saucepan. Remove the garlic from the saucepan and add
the tomatoes, a generous sprinkle of salt and pepper, and the squids.
Cover the pan and simmer for 10 minutes. Add the black olives,
raisins, pine nuts, and water. Cover the pan and cook for another 10
minutes, or until the squids are tender. Arrange slices of toast in
serving bowls, and spoon the squids and sauce over the toast just
before serving.

Serves 4.

Stuffed Littleneck Clams

3 lb/1350 g littleneck clams
2 small splashes of white wine
3/4 cup/175 ml unsalted butter
2 garlic cloves, pasted
2 Tbsp/30 ml fresh tarragon, chopped (or parsley if you prefer)
2 handfuls fresh breadcrumbs
2 pinches salt

Place the clams and the wine into a large saucepan with a tight-fitting lid and steam until open. When they have cooled, remove the empty shell from the clams and place the bottom shell containing the clam meat side by side on a serving dish. Add the butter, the garlic, and the tarragon to the remaining juices in the pan and allow the flavours to infuse for 2-3 minutes, then add the breadcrumbs until all the juices have been soaked up. Place a teaspoon on the top of each clam. Finish under a hot grill until crisp and serve with a squeeze of lemon juice.

Serves 3.

Broiled Cod with Olive Paste

2 lb/1 kg fresh cod fillets
1/4 cup/50 ml kalamata olives, chopped
1/4 cup/50 ml spanish olives, chopped
2 tsp/10 ml capers
1 1/2 tsp/7 ml anchovies (about 2), minced
2 – 3 tsp/10 to 15 ml garlic, minced
1 1/2 Tbsp/22 ml olive oil
1 Tbsp/15 ml balsamic vinegar
1/3 cup/75 ml tomatoes, diced
2 Tbsp/30 ml fresh parsley (optional), chopped
salt and pepper to taste

Preheat the broiler.

Mix together the olives, capers, anchovies, garlic, 1 Tbsp/15 ml of the olive oil, the balsamic vinegar, tomatoes, and parsley, in a medium bowl. Season with salt and pepper to taste.

Coat the cod fillets on both sides with the remaining olive oil. Place in a broiling pan, and broil for 8 to 10 minutes, or until cooked through. It is unnecessary to turn the fish—the heat of the pan will cook the bottom side. Remove from the pan and spoon the olive mixture over the fillets.

Serves 4.

Cod or Salmon Fish Cakes

1 lb/455 g mixed fresh fish fillets, such as cod and salmon, skinned
1 lb/455 g potatoes, such as Russet, peeled and cut into chunks
2 Tbsp/30 ml fresh tarragon, chopped

grated zest of 1 lemon
2 Tbsp/30 ml heavy cream
1 Tbsp/15 ml flour
1 egg, beaten
1 cup/250 ml bread crumbs
1/4 cup/50 ml olive oil
salt and pepper to taste
lemon wedges, to garnish

Bring a large pan of salted water to a boil, add the potatoes, and cook for 15-20 minutes. Drain well, then mash until smooth.

Put the fish in a skillet and just cover with water. Bring to a boil over medium heat, then reduce the heat to low, cover, and let simmer gently for 5 minutes or until cooked.

Remove with a slotted spoon and drain on a plate. When cool enough to handle, flake the fish coarsely into good-sized pieces, removing any bones.

Mix the mashed potatoes with the fish, tarragon, lemon zest, and cream in a bowl. Season well with salt and pepper and shape into 4 round cakes or 8 smaller ones with your hands.

Put the flour, egg, and bread crumbs in separate bowls. Dust the fish cakes with flour, dip into the beaten egg, then coat thoroughly in the bread crumbs. Put on a baking sheet, cover, and refrigerate for at least 30 minutes.

Heat the oil in the skillet over medium heat, add the fish cakes, and cook for 5 minutes on each side

Garnish with lemon wedges and serve hot.

Serves 4.

Grilled Cod with Caper-Parsley Sauce

4 fresh cod fillets or steaks, 8 oz/225 g each
1 Tbsp/15 ml olive oil
salt and pepper to taste
caper-parsley sauce

Preheat barbeque to medium-high heat 425°F/220°C. Brush the fish lightly with the olive oil and sprinkle with salt and pepper.

Grill until opaque and just beginning to flake when tested with a fork, about 10 minutes per inch of thickness, turning once halfway through the cooking time.

Serves 4.

Caper-Parsley Sauce

This sauce goes well with all shellfish. It also makes a delicious pasta sauce.

3 Tbsp/45 ml white wine vinegar
1 cup/250 ml fresh parsley, chopped
2 garlic cloves, minced

1/4 cup/50 ml tiny capers, drained
1 Tbsp/15 ml onion, chopped
1 Tbsp/15 ml Dijon mustard
2/3 cup/150 ml olive oil

Place the vinegar, parsley, garlic, capers, onion, and mustard in a food processor or blender and process until smooth. While the machine is running, add the olive oil slowly in a thin stream through the feed tube to make a thick, green sauce. Chill until ready to serve. This will keep, tightly covered, in the refrigerator for several days.

Makes 1 1/2 cups/375 ml.

Alaskan King Crab

2 lb/1 kg fresh king crab legs
1/2 cup /125 ml butter
1/4 cup /50 ml lemon juice
1/4 cup/50 ml dry white wine
1 Tbsp/15 ml scallions or chives, finely chopped

Prepare the butter dip by melting the butter in a small saucepan and adding the lemon juice, wine, and scallions or chives. Cook over low heat for a couple of minutes. Keep warm.

Alaskan King Crab is shipped to market parboiled and only needs 5 minutes of cooking time to complete cooking.

Split the crab legs with a knife and open both sides to face towards broiler elements in stove. Broil in oven for 5 minutes. Remove. Pour butter dip generously over crab meat and enjoy!

Be sure to supply claw crackers and seafood forks.

Serves 4.

*A woman without a man is like a
fish without a bicycle.*

–Gloria Steinem

Crab Salad Louis

1 lb/455 g fresh crabmeat, picked over for shells and cartilage
1/2 to 3/4 cup/125 to 175 ml mayonnaise
2 Tbsp/30 ml ketchup
1/4 tsp/1 ml horseradish
1/8 tsp/1/2 ml Dijon mustard
1 Tbsp/15 ml onion, minced
1 Tbsp/15 ml fresh parsley, finely chopped or 1/2 Tbsp/2 ml fresh
    sweet marjoram, chopped
mixed romaine lettuce and radicchio
fresh lemon juice
1 avocado, peeled and sliced
2 hard-boiled eggs, sliced

Mix together the mayonnaise, ketchup, horseradish, mustard, onion,
and parsley. Let sit for at least 20 minutes to let the flavours meld.
On a large circular platter, arrange the greens in a circle around the
edge, leaving the centre open. Place the crabmeat in the centre.
Drizzle the mayonnaise sauce over the crabmeat. Squeeze lemon
juice to taste over the avocado slices and use as a garnish along with
the hard-boiled eggs.

Serves 2.

Baked Tomato Grouper

4 fresh grouper steaks,
  8 oz/250 g each
1 cup/250 ml fish stock, heated
1 Tbsp/15 ml olive oil
2 small onions, sliced
1 garlic clove, minced

4 small tomatoes, peeled, cored
  and quartered
4 tsp/20 ml Dijon mustard
1/4 tsp/1 ml fennel seed
salt and pepper to taste

Preheat oven to 375°F – 400°F/190°C – 200°C. Heat oil in a frying pan over medium heat. Add onions and garlic; cook 5 minutes. Stir once during cooking.

Add tomatoes and season well. Cover and continue cooking 5 minutes.

Spread mustard over grouper steaks. Place fish in ovenproof baking dish and cover with tomato mixture. Pour in fish stock and sprinkle with fennel seed.

Cook 10 to 15 minutes in oven.

Serves 4.

Our disputants put me in mind of the skuttle fish, that when he is unable to extricate himself, blackens all the water about him, till he becomes invisible.

–Joseph Addison, *The Spectator*

Haddock Pie

1 1/2 lb/680 g fresh haddock
    fillets
Sauce Béchamel (page 29)
5 medium-size potatoes, boiled
    and mashed with butter and
    milk
slice of lemon
1 small onion, finely chopped

1 or 2 egg yolks, beaten
2 eggs, hardboiled and chopped
1/2 english cucumber, unpeeled
    and diced
pie pastry
tarragon
salt and pepper to taste

Poach haddock in water with lemon slice and allow to cool in the
cooking liquid. Flake and mix with Sauce Béchamel, chopped
hardboiled egg, diced cucumber, onion, and seasonings to taste.
Butter a pie dish and line the sides with pastry. Spread a layer of
mashed potatoes, followed by a layer of half the fish mixture, and
repeat. Roll out the rest of the pastry and cover the pie. Make two
slits on the top and brush the crust with beaten egg yolk. Bake at
375°F – 400°F/190°C – 200°C until pastry is golden brown, reduce
heat to 225°F/105°C, and continue baking 15 minutes.

Serves 4.

Healthy Haddock Stew

2 lb/1 kg fresh haddock, rinsed and cubed
5 bacon slices, diced
1/2 red onion, chopped
2 garlic cloves, smashed and chopped
4 potatoes, peeled and diced
4 cups/1 L vegetable stock, heated
2 fresh fennel sprigs
2 Tbsp/30 ml butter
2 Tbsp/30 ml flour
1 Tbsp/15 ml fresh parsley, chopped
salt and pepper to taste

Cook bacon 6 minutes in a large saucepan over medium heat. Add onion and garlic. Reduce heat to low and cook 4 minutes.

Stir in potatoes, vegetable stock and fresh fennel. Season well and cook 12 minutes over low heat.

Add fish and cook 6 minutes. Discard fennel sprigs. Remove 1 cup/250 ml of cooking liquid and set aside.

Heat butter in another saucepan over medium heat. Sprinkle in flour and mix well. Cook 15 seconds. Incorporate reserved cooking liquid. Pour mixture into pan containing fish and vegetables; mix gently. Add parsley and serve.

Serves 4.

Barbecued Marinated Halibut

4 fresh halibut steaks, 8 oz/225 g each
3 Tbsp/45 m peanut oil   *Od*
1 Tbsp/15 ml sesame oil
2 Tbsp/30 ml soy sauce
2 Tbsp/30 ml honey
3 garlic cloves, finely chopped
1/4 cup/50 ml chicken stock
juice of 1/2 lemon
pepper to taste

Place halibut steaks in a roasting pan and season with pepper. In a bowl, mix together peanut oil, sesame oil, soy sauce, honey, garlic, chicken stock, and lemon juice.

Pour mixture over fish and marinate 1 hour. Turn and marinate 1 hour or more.

Grill fish on preheated medium-high barbecue 6 to 7 minutes on each side, or adjust time depending on thickness. Baste frequently during cooking.

Serve fish with vegetable rice and zucchini, if desired.

Serves 4.

Halibut Salad

A great change from tuna!

1 lb/455 g fresh halibut fillet, about 3/4" thick
4 Tbsp/60 ml olive oil
1/2 cup/125 ml mayonnaise
2 stalks celery, finely chopped
3 scallions (white parts only), chopped
3 sprigs fresh dill, chopped
salt and pepper

Lightly coat a medium-sized frying pan with oil and heat over medium-high heat. Sear halibut fillet until browned, 3–5 minutes per side. Allow halibut to cool, then flake into large pieces and set aside.

Mix together mayonnaise, celery, scallions, and dill in a medium bowl and season to taste with salt and pepper. Fold in flaked fish and adjust seasonings. Use as a sandwich filling or serve as a salad.

Serves 2.

Un-dish-cover the fish, or dishcover the riddle.

—Lewis Carroll, *Through the Looking-Glass*

Italian Baked Halibut

4 fresh halibut steaks, 8 oz/225 g each
1 onion, sliced
1 small green pepper, chopped
1 10 oz/285 ml can peeled tomatoes
1/4 cup/50 ml raisins
1/4 cup/50 ml white wine
6 medium mushrooms, thinly sliced
3 Tbsp/45 ml butter
1/2 tsp/2 ml oregano
juice of a lemon
flour
paprika
bay leaf
salt and pepper to taste

Sauté onions and green pepper in 1 Tbsp/15 ml butter, but do not
brown. Add tomatoes, oregano, bay leaf, mushrooms, salt, and
pepper. Cook over medium heat about 15 minutes. Set aside. Roll
the halibut steaks in a mixture of flour and paprika. In a frying pan,
brown them on both sides in butter. Place halibut in a baking dish.
Sprinkle with raisins, lemon juice, and wine. Pour sauce over top,
bake uncovered in a preheated oven at 375°F – 400°F/190°C –
200°C about 10 to 15 minutes. Check with fork to see if cooked.
Colour will be uniform throughout.

Serves 4.

Nutty Halibut

2 lb/1 kg fresh halibut fillet
4 Tbsp/60 ml butter, melted
1/2 cup/125 ml pistachios, shelled and very finely chopped

Brush the melted butter over the halibut fillet. Spread the nuts out on a large, flat plate. Roll the fish in the nuts, pressing down gently. Preheat the griddle or a stovetop grill pan over medium-high heat. Cook the halibut, turning once, for 10 minutes, or until firm but tender—the exact cooking time will depend on the thickness of the fillet. Remove the fish from the heat and transfer to a large, warmed serving platter. Serve at once.

Serves 4.

The sea hath fish for every man.

–William Camden, *Remains Concerning Britain*

Lapointe's Paella

8 oz/225 g squid, cleaned and sliced
one 1 1/2 to 2 lb/680 g to 1 kg lobster, cut into pieces
10 mussels, cleaned
6 small littleneck clams, cleaned
12 raw medium shrimp, cleaned
1/2 frying chicken, cut into 4 pieces, washed, and patted dry
1/4 lb/115 g veal, cut into cubes
1/2 medium onion, chopped
1/2 large red bell pepper, chopped
1 garlic clove, minced
1 cup/250 ml long-grain rice
pinch saffron, toasted for minute in a dry pan to release flavour
2 1/2 cups/625 ml chicken stock, simmering
1/4 cup/50 ml olive oil
1/4 cup/50 ml string beans, blanched
1/4 cup/50 ml green peas, defrosted
2 small jars red pimentos, sliced into 1-inch-thick pieces
1/2 tsp/2 ml salt and freshly ground black pepper
1 lemon, cut into wedges

Preheat the oven to 450°F/230°C

Set a paella pan or large ovenproof skillet over high heat, add the
olive oil, and, when the oil is hot, add the chicken and the veal.
Brown the meat on all sides, turning often, 5 to 8 minutes. Add the
onion, bell pepper, garlic, and squid. Cook, stirring the ingredients,
until they are all slightly brown, about 5 minutes. Stir in the rice,
saffron, salt, and pepper, making sure the rice is coated with the oil.
Pour in the stock and bring to a boil.

Add the lobster, mussels, clams, and shrimp. Bring the mixture back
to the boil, add the beans and peas, and arrange the pimentos on
top. Transfer the pan to the oven and bake until the seafood is
cooked, about 25 minutes. Bring the paella to the table in its pan
and serve with lemon wedges.

Serves 4.

Lobster Cakes

1 tin of frozen lobster, thawed with bits of cartilage removed
1/4 cup/50 ml each celery and green onion, finely diced
small handful of parsley, chopped
capers, drained, chopped (optional)
juice of one lemon at room temperature
1 egg, beaten
dash Tabasco
pinch of thyme and dill
shred one peeled, baked potato
2 Tbsp/30 ml of mayonnaise
some crushed soda crackers
salt and pepper to taste

Mix all and refrigerate till cold. Shape into cake patties. Dredge in flour and pan fry, or dredge in breadcrumbs, place on a parchment paper-lined cookie sheet, brush some melted butter over cakes, and bake at 400°–425°F /200°–220°C for about 10 minutes.

Chef's suggestions: The cakes are great served with roasted red pepper mayo. Roast one red pepper in a hot oven or over barbecue till charred, then place in a paper bag for a few minutes, peel skin off, and zap in a food processor with a little mayonnaise.

Serves 2.

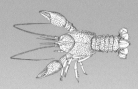

Lobster Francois

1 live lobster, about 2 lb/1 kg
1 tsp/5 ml sesame seeds
1 tsp/5 ml onion salt
1 tsp/5 ml poppy seeds
1 Tbsp/15 ml chives, chopped
1/4 tsp to 1/2 tsp garlic salt
1/2 tsp/2 ml oregano
1/2 tsp/2 ml thyme
1/4 tsp/1 ml black pepper
2 Tbsp/30 ml butter
1 Tbsp/15 ml port wine
breadcrumbs
Romano cheese

Cook lobster (see instructions in the "Lobster" section). Cut in half
lengthwise, remove sac behind head, and discard. Mix all seasonings
except breadcrumbs, butter, and wine; sprinkle the seasoning
mixture over each half. Sprinkle with bread crumbs, and top with
grated Romano cheese and butter. Broil two minutes. Sprinkle with
wine and return to broiler for one minute. Garnish and serve.

Serves 2.

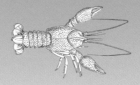

Lobster Mornay

1 2 to 3 lb/1 kg to 1350 g
  Lobster, cooked
1 1/4 cups/300 ml milk
1 onion, sliced
1 bay leaf
6 black peppercorns

2 Tbsp/30 ml butter
2 Tbsp/30 ml flour
pinch of nutmeg
2 Tbsp/30 ml cream
1/2 cup/125 ml grated cheddar
salt to taste

Using a sharp knife, cut the lobster in half lengthways. Lift the meat from the tail and body. Crack the legs and remove the meat. Remove the intestinal vein and soft body matter and discard. Cut the meat into bite-sized pieces, cover, and refrigerate. Wash the shell halves, drain, and dry.

Heat the milk, onion, bay leaf, and peppercorns in a small pan. Bring to the boil then remove from the heat, cover and leave for 15 minutes. Strain.

Melt the butter in a large pan, add the flour, and stir for 1 minute. Remove from the heat and gradually add the infused milk. Stir until smooth. Cook, stirring over medium heat, until the mixture boils and thickens. Season with salt, pepper, and nutmeg. Stir in the cream.

Fold the lobster meat through the sauce. Divide the mixture between the shells and sprinkle the top with the cheese. Place under a preheated grill for 2 minutes, or until the cheese has melted.

Serves 2.

Lobster Newburg

2 lb/1 kg cooked lobster
1/2 cup/125 ml Madeira wine
1/2 cup/125 ml cream
2 egg yolks
1/4 cup/50 ml butter
salt and pepper to taste

Remove all meat from body and claws. Cut lobster into chunks about 1 to 1-1/2 inches /2.5 to 3.8 cm wide. Arrange meat in a well-buttered sauté pan, add a little salt and pepper, and heat through, turning once. Add wine and reduce the volume about two-thirds by sautéing. Just before serving, add blended egg yolks and cream. Do not allow the sauce to boil. Draw pan to side of burner and add butter a little at a time, stirring constantly. As the yolks cook, the sauce will thicken. Serve in a lobster-shaped dish accompanied by rice pilaf and topped with a puff pastry.

Serves 2.

Immense, of fishy form and mind,
Squamous, omnipotent, and kind;
And under that Almighty Fin,
The littlest fish may enter in.

–Rupert Brooke, *Heaven*

Lobster Thermidor

4 cooked lobsters, 1 1/2 lbs/
  680 g each
1 onion
1 bay leaf
8 black peppercorns, whole
2 cups/500 ml milk
4 Tbsp/60 ml unsalted butter

1 Tbsp/15 ml flour
1 tsp/5 ml Dijon mustard
2 garlic cloves, crushed
1 shot of brandy
handful of fresh tarragon leaves,
  chopped
salt and pepper to taste

Remove all meat from body and claws. Keep the shells for serving.

Make the sauce base by placing the onion, bay leaf, peppercorns, and milk into a pan and bringing to the boil. Simmer for 1-3 minutes and remove from the heat and leave to one side to infuse – about 10 minutes.

In another pan, gently melt half the butter and stir in the flour to make a roux (a thick, creamy paste). Take off the heat and slowly add the cooled milk, stirring all the time to avoid lumps, and allow the sauce to thicken. Return to the heat and gently warm to cook the flour and let the sauce thicken. Stir in the mustard and set aside. If you find that you have any lumps, simply strain the sauce through a sieve.

In a larger pan, add the rest of the butter and gently sauté the garlic, allowing the butter to become well-flavoured. Add all the lobster meat, stirring it around so that it becomes coated in the garlic and butter. Pour in the brandy and set alight until the alcohol is burned off. Pour in the sauce base and add the tarragon. Stir and season to taste. Place this mixture back in the shells and place under a hot broiler for 1-2 minutes until golden on top.

Serves 4.

Mahi Mahi Amandine

4 fresh mahi mahi fillets,
   8 oz/225 g each
1 garlic clove, minced
1/2 cup/125 ml olive oil
1/4 cup/50 ml slivered almonds
2 Tbsp/30 ml butter

2 Tbsp/30 ml parsley, finely
   chopped
juice of 1/2 lemon
a few drops of lemon juice
salt and pepper to taste

Rinse and pat mahi mahi fillets dry with a towel. Sprinkle with salt and pepper. Mix garlic, juice of 1/2 lemon, and oil in a bowl. Add mahi mahi and marinate for 30 minutes. Using a small frying pan, make almond topping by sautéing slivered almonds in butter until light golden brown. Stir in minced parsley and a few drops of lemon juice and remove from heat. Remove mahi mahi from marinade. Put fillets on a greased, heated grill, ensuring the pieces don't touch each other. Brush fish frequently with the marinade. Grill 4–5 minutes on each side. Cook until mahi mahi flakes easily. Spoon almond topping over grilled fish and serve immediately.

Serves 4.

Well, Mr. Baldwin! this is a pretty kettle of fish!

–Queen Mary, during the abdication crisis, 1936

Mahi Mahi Baked with Bacon

4 fresh mahi steaks,
   8 oz/225 g each
4 slices bacon
1 1/2 cups/375 ml tomatoes
   peeled, seeded, and diced
1/4 cup/50 ml red or green

pepper, diced
1/2 cup/125 ml onions,
   chopped
1 tsp/5 ml olive oil
pepper to taste

Oil a baking pan just large enough to hold the fish. Mix together the tomatoes, pepper, onions, and olive oil. Place the fish fillets in the pan, skin side down, and sprinkle with pepper. Top with the tomato mixture. Arrange the bacon on top. Bake for 12 to 15 minutes, or until the fish is cooked through.

Serves 4.

How cheerfully he seems to grin,
How neatly spreads his claws,
And welcomes little fishes in
With gently smiling jaws!

–from "How doth the little crocodile" in Lewis Carroll's
Alice's Adventures in Wonderland

Mahi Mahi with Basil Butter

4 fresh mahi mahi fillets,
   8 oz/225 g each
Basil Butter:
1 cup/250 ml butter
1/2 cup/125 ml fresh basil,
   chopped

Marinade:
1 cup/250 ml olive oil
1/4 tsp/1 ml ground white
   pepper
1/4 tsp/1 ml salt
1/4 tsp/1 ml garlic powder
juice of one lemon

Marinate fillets for one hour at room temperature in olive oil, white
pepper, salt, garlic powder, and lemon juice. Using a food processor,
cream the butter with the basil to serve on the side with mahi mahi.
Grill the fillets for 4–5 minutes on each side and serve immediately.

Serves 4.

*No human being, however great or powerful,
was ever so free as a fish.*

–John Ruskin, Lecture v

Mahi Mahi with Ginger and Lime

4 fresh mahi mahi steaks,
  8 oz/225 g each
3 garlic cloves, crushed
1 Tbsp/15 ml fresh ginger, grated
1 tsp/5 ml sugar
1/2 tsp/2 ml dried crushed red
  pepper

3 Tbsp/45 ml fresh lime juice
2 Tbsp/30 ml low-sodium soy
  sauce
1 Tbsp/15 ml dark sesame oil

Place steaks in a large, shallow dish. Combine garlic and remaining ingredients in a small bowl. Stir well. Pour marinade mixture over steaks. Cover and marinate in refrigerator 1 hour, turning once.

Remove steaks from marinade, reserving marinade. Bring marinade to a boil in a small saucepan. Grill steaks 4–5 minutes per side until fish flakes easily when tested with a fork, turning once and basting often with marinade.

Serves 4.

Barbequed Balsamic-Glazed Marlin Steaks

2 fresh marlin steaks, 8 oz/225 g each
3 Tbsp/45 ml unsalted butter
1/3 cup/75 ml balsamic vinegar
salt and lemon pepper to taste

Preheat barbeque to medium-high heat 425°F/220°C.

Meanwhile, season the steaks with salt and lemon pepper. Let stand at room temperature for 10 to 15 minutes.

In a small saucepan, melt the butter and whisk in the balsamic vinegar to make a glaze. Set aside.

Grill the steaks on an oiled grill rack until they are opaque and just beginning to flake when tested with a fork, about 5 minutes per side, turning once and basting with the glaze.

Also good with: shark, swordfish, or tuna.

Serves 2.

Barbecued Monkfish Kabobs

2 lb/1 kg fresh monkfish fillet, cut into chunks
4 Tbsp/60 ml olive oil
zest of 1 lime
2 tsp/10 ml Thai fish sauce
2 garlic cloves, crushed
1 tsp/5 ml fresh ginger, grated
2 Tbsp/30 ml fresh basil, chopped
2 limes, cut into 6 wedges
salt and pepper
fresh basil leaves, to garnish
freshly cooked noodles, to serve

Mix the olive oil, lime zest, Thai fish sauce, garlic, ginger, and basil together. Season to taste with salt and pepper and set aside.

Wash the fish under cold running water and pat dry with paper towels. Add to the marinade and mix well. Cover and let marinate in the refrigerator for 2 hours, stirring occasionally.

If you are using bamboo skewers, soak them in cold water for 30 minutes. Lift the monkfish pieces from the marinade and thread them onto the skewers, alternating with the lime wedges.

Transfer the skewers to a lit barbecue and cook for 5–6 minutes, turning regularly, until the fish is tender. Pile freshly cooked noodles onto 4 large, warmed serving plates and put the monkfish kabobs on top. Garnish with a few fresh basil leaves and serve.

Serves 4.

Monkfish Tail with Grapefruit

2 lb/1 kg fresh monkfish tail
2 Tbsp/30 ml olive oil
1 cup/250 ml grapefruit juice
2 Tbsp/30 ml sugar
1 tsp/5 ml chopped ginger in syrup
A few drops hot pepper sauce
1/4 cup/50 ml cold unsalted butter cut in small pieces
1 cup/250 ml ruby red grapefruit segments
2 Tbsp/30 ml mint, finely chopped
salt and pepper to taste

Preheat oven to 375°F – 400°F/190°C – 200°C.

Cut monkfish into 1-inch medallions. Season fish with salt and pepper. Heat oil in an ovenproof skillet over medium heat. Add fish and fry for 2 minutes per side or until brown. Place in oven and bake 5 minutes or until just cooked through. Remove fish to plate and keep warm. Discard any oil.

Add grapefruit juice, sugar, and ginger to skillet. Bring to boil and boil until slightly syrupy, about 3 to 5 minutes. Sprinkle in hot pepper sauce. Add any fish juice from the fish.

Reduce heat to low and whisk in butter. Sauce will thicken. Stir in grapefruit segments and mint.

Divide sauce between 4 serving plates and top with fish.

Serves 4.

Stuffed Monkfish Tail

2 lb/1 kg fresh monkfish tail, skinned and trimmed
8 slices prosciutto
4 Tbsp/60 ml mixed herbs such as parsley, chives, basil, and sage,
  chopped
1 tsp/5 ml lemon zest
1/4 cup/50 ml olive oil
salt and pepper to taste

Using a sharp knife, carefully cut down each side of the central bone of the monkfish to leave 2 fillets. Wash the fillets under cold running water and pat dry with paper towels.

Lay the prosciutto slices widthwise on a clean counter so that they overlap slightly. Lay the fish fillets lengthwise on top of the prosciutto so that the two cut sides face each other.

Mix the chopped herbs and lemon rind together. Season well with salt and pepper. Pack this mixture onto the cut surface of one monkfish fillet. Press the two fillets together and wrap tightly with the prosciutto slices. Secure with string or toothpicks.

Heat the olive oil in a large, heavy-based skillet. Place the fish in the skillet, seam side down first, and brown the wrapped monkfish tail all over.

Cook in a preheated oven, 375°F – 400°F/190°C – 200°C, for approximately 15 minutes until golden and the fish is tender. Remove from the oven and let rest for 5 minutes before slicing thickly. Serve with stir-fried vegetables and new potatoes.

Serves 4.

Moules Marinière

48 mussels, well scrubbed
3 cups/750 ml white wine
1 medium-size onion, finely chopped
4 garlic cloves, finely chopped
4 whole fresh basil leaves, or 2 Tbsp/30 ml dried basil
3 parsley sprigs
1 tbsp/15 ml fresh lemon juice
1/4 cup/50 ml butter
4 tsp/20 ml parsley, finely chopped
1 tsp/5 ml coarse salt
1 tsp/5 ml coarse black pepper

Place the mussels in a large kettle with all ingredients except the butter and minced parsley. Bring to a boil, then cover and simmer until the mussels have opened. Remove the bivalves with a slotted spoon, discarding any that have not opened. Add butter to the liquid and raise the heat to reduce the liquid by half. In the meantime, arrange the mussels in their open shells in warm bowls or soup plates. When the liquid is reduced, pass it through a fine sieve into a smaller pan, then warm again over low heat and pour some directly over each portion of mussels. Sprinkle 1 tsp/5 ml parsley over each serving. Accompany with crisp French bread.

Serves 4.

Moules Provençale

Follow the recipe for Moules Marinière, but substitute 1 1/2 cups/750 ml red wine and 1 1/2 cups/750 ml tomato purée for the white wine. In addition to the parsley, grate parmesan cheese over the mussels.

Serves 4.

Mussels au Gratin

5 lbs/2.25 kg cleaned mussels
1/4 cup/50 ml garlic, chopped
1 cup/250 ml butter
1/2 cup/125 ml fresh parsley,
  chopped
1 cup/250 ml dry white wine
1 medium onion, chopped
  (about 1 cup/250 ml)

3/4 to 1 cup/175 to 250 ml
  freshly grated medium
  cheese
2 cups/500 ml seasoned bread
  crumbs
lemon wedges
French bread

Preheat the oven to 375°F – 400°F/190°C – 200°C

Cream together 2 tbsp/30 ml of the garlic, the butter, and the parsley in a small bowl. Set aside.

Put the wine, the remaining garlic, and the onions in a large pot. Bring the mixture to a boil, then add the mussels. Reduce the heat to medium, cover the pot, and steam the mussels until they open, about 6 minutes. Stir them occasionally. Remove the mussels with a slotted spoon the moment their shells open, because they lose flavour if overcooked. Break off the top shell. Centre each mussel in its shell, and place on a baking pan or in a large baking dish.

Reduce the mussel broth over high heat until the flavour is concentrated and pour it around the mussels in the pan. Put 1 tsp/5 ml of the garlic butter in each mussel shell. Sprinkle with the cheese, and pat the crumb mixture over the cheese. Bake for about 10 minutes, or until the crumb topping is lightly browned. Serve the mussels immediately, garnished with lemon wedges and accompanied by French bread to soak up the pan juices.

Serves 5.

Mussels in Saffron Broth

4 lbs/2 kg mussels
1/4 cup/50 ml heavy whipping cream
1/2 cup/125 ml fresh chives or green onions, chopped
1/2 cup/125 ml butter
1 cup/250 ml shallots (about 4 large), finely chopped
8 garlic cloves, chopped
2 Tbsp/30 ml fresh thyme, chopped
2 cups/500 ml dry white wine
3 Tbsp/45 ml Dijon mustard
1/2 tsp/2 ml saffron threads
salt and pepper to taste

Melt butter in heavy large pot over medium-high heat. Add shallots, garlic, and thyme; season with pepper. Sauté until shallots are soft, about 5 minutes. Mix in wine and mustard. Boil 2 minutes. Add saffron. Remove from heat and let steep 5 minutes. (Can be made one hour ahead. Let stand at room temperature.)

Add cream and mussels to pot and return to boil. Cover and cook until mussels open, about 6 minutes. Mix in chives. Season broth to taste with salt and pepper. Divide mussels and broth among 6 shallow bowls (discard any mussels that do not open) and serve.

Soak up remaining juice with French bread such as baguettes.

Serves 4.

Oven-Roasted Mussels

4 lbs/2 kg cleaned mussels
2 Tbsp/30 ml garlic, chopped
1 cup/250 ml onions, chopped
1 Tbsp/15 ml olive oil

Preheat the oven to 400°F/200°C.

Place the garlic, onion, and oil in a large baking dish. Top with the mussels. Roast for 10 to 12 minutes, or until the mussels open completely. Discard any that do not open. Serve immediately with the mussel liquor on the side.

Serves 4.

When thirsty grief in wine we steep,
When healths and draughts go free,
Fishes, that tipple in the deep,
Know no such liberty.

–Richard Lovelace, "To Althea, From Prison"

Broiled Oysters with Chicken Livers

24 fresh shucked oysters
12 chicken livers
7 Tbsp/105 ml butter
4 slices of bacon
4 slices of crisp toast

1 tsp/5 ml lemon juice
2 tsp/30 ml parsley, chopped
lemon wedges
salt and pepper to taste

Drain oysters, saving the juice. Sauté livers slightly in 3 Tbsp/45 ml of the butter seasoned with salt and pepper. Cook the bacon until crisp and set aside. Skewer livers and oysters alternately and broil until the oysters curl. Cover each slice of toast with livers and oysters. Make a sauce in the sauté pan by adding oyster juice to taste, the lemon juice and remaining butter. Pour this over oysters and garnish with bacon, parsley, and lemon wedges.

Serves 4.

Grilled Oysters in Pesto

24 fresh oysters on the half shell
pesto — see pesto on page 30.
chopped fresh plum tomatoes and black olives for garnish

Preheat barbeque to medium-high.

Arrange the oysters in a single layer on an oiled perforated grill rack.
Spoon about 1 tsp/5 ml of the pesto over each oyster. Place the
oysters on the grill, cover, and grill until the pesto is bubbling and the
edges of the oysters have begun to curl, 3 to 5 minutes.

Serve immediately with the chopped tomatoes and olives sprinkled
on top for garnish.

Serves 4.

Summertime and the living is easy,
Fish are jumping, and the cotton is high.

–Ira Gershwin, song "Summertime"

Oysters Kilpatrick

24 fresh oysters on the half shell
2 Tbsp/30 ml butter
2 Tbsp/30 ml Worcestershire sauce

3 slices of bacon, finely
chopped
black pepper to taste

Place oysters in half shells on a grill tray. Heat butter in a small pan. Add Worcestershire sauce and simmer for 2 minutes. Spoon half a teaspoon/2 ml of the sauce onto each oyster. Sprinkle with bacon and some ground black pepper. Grill for 3–4 minutes, or until the bacon is crisp. Serve immediately on a bed of rock salt.

Serves 4.

Oysters Mornay

24 fresh oysters on the half shell
2 Tbsp/30 ml butter
1 Tbsp/15 ml flour
2/3 cup/150 ml hot milk
pinch of cayenne pepper

1 Tbsp/15 ml cream
1/3 cup/75 ml grated cheddar
paprika, to sprinkle
salt and pepper to taste

Melt the butter in a small pan. Stir in the flour and cook for 2 minutes. Remove from the heat and gradually stir in the hot milk. Stir over medium heat until the mixture boils and thickens. Season with salt, pepper, and the cayenne pepper.

Simmer the sauce very gently for 2 minutes, stirring occasionally. Stir in the cream. Remove from the heat and lay baking paper directly on the surface to prevent a skin forming.

Drain the juice from the oysters and add the juice to the sauce. Arrange the oysters in shells on a bed of rock salt on a baking or grill tray. Top the oysters with a tsp/5 ml of the hot sauce and sprinkle with the cheese. Place under a hot grill for 2–3 minutes, or until lightly browned. Sprinkle with the paprika.

Serves 4.

Oysters Rockefeller

24 fresh oysters on the half shell
2 Tbsp/30 ml butter
2 slices of bacon, finely chopped
8 spinach leaves, finely chopped
2 Tbsp/30 ml each of parsley and green onion, chopped
1/3 cup/75 ml dry breadcrumbs
dash Tabasco

Arrange oysters in half shells on rock salt. Cover and refrigerate. Melt butter in a pan and cook bacon over medium heat until browned. Add finely chopped spinach leaves, parsley, and green onion, breadcrumbs, and a dash of Tabasco. Cook for 5 minutes, or until the spinach wilts. Spoon a little over each oyster and grill for 2–3 minutes, or until lightly browned.

Serves 4.

I have other fish to fry.

—Cervantes, *Don Quixote*

Baked Red Snapper Amandine

2 lb/1 kg fresh red snapper fillets
1/4 cup/50 ml olive oil
1/2 cup/125 ml almonds, slivered & blanched
1/2 cup/125 ml melted butter
juice of 1 small lemon
salt and pepper to taste

Wipe red snapper fillets with a damp cloth. Season with salt and pepper and dredge with flour. Sauté the fillets in olive oil until they are nicely browned on both sides. Lay the fillets in a large baking dish and pour over them the following mixture: almonds, melted butter, and lemon juice. Bake in a hot oven for 8 to 10 minutes, or until the almonds are nicely browned.

Serves 4.

Baked Red Snapper
in Orange Sauce

2 lb/1 kg fresh red snapper fillets
3 Tbsp/45 ml olive oil
2 Tbsp/30 ml orange juice
2 tsp/10 ml orange zest
1 tsp/5 ml salt
dash of nutmeg
dash of pepper

Cut the snapper fillets into serving-size portions. Place in a single layer, skin side down, in a large well-greased baking dish. Combine remaining ingredients and pour over fish. Bake in a preheated oven (375°F – 400°F/190°C – 200°C) for 8 to 10 minutes, or until fish flakes easily when tested with a fork.

Serves 4.

Barbecued Red Snapper

2 lb/1 kg fresh red snapper fillets
1/2 cup/125 ml tomato juice
1 Tbsp/15 ml olive oil
2 Tbsp/30 ml lemon juice
1/2 tsp/2 ml salt
1 garlic clove, minced
1 tsp/5 ml salt
1 tsp/5 ml fennel seed
1 tsp/5 ml ginger

Place the snapper fillets in a shallow pan. Mix together the remaining ingredients and pour over the fish. Marinate for 2 hours in refrigerator. Drain, reserving the marinade. Barbecue over medium-high heat for approximately 8–10 minutes, brushing occasionally and turning once.

Serves 4.

Braised Salmon with Wine

4 fresh salmon steaks (about 1/2 lb/225 g each)
3 shallots, chopped
10 medium-size white mushrooms
1 1/4 cup/300 ml cream
1/2 cup/125 ml butter
1/2 cup/125 ml dry white wine
salt and pepper to taste
parsley

Butter a heat-proof dish, add salmon steaks, shallots, and sliced mushrooms (bake four heads whole for decoration). Add salt and pepper and wine and bake in medium oven for 12 to 15 minutes, according to thickness of steaks.

Remove salmon steaks and mushroom heads from oven. Carefully remove skin and bones. Cover and keep warm.

Reduce juice by half. Combine with creamed butter and cream and continue reducing until sauce is smooth and creamy. Check seasoning and strain through fine strainer.

Just before serving, place salmon steaks on an oval dish, put a mushroom head on each and cover with sauce. Decorate with parsley. Serve hot.

Serves 4.

Honey-Lime
Salmon Kebabs

3 lbs/1350 g fresh salmon fillet, skin on, cut into 1"/2.5 cm chunks
1 green bell pepper, cut into 1"/2.5 cm squares
1 red onion, cut into 1"/2.5 cm squares
2 cups/500 ml halved mushrooms
1 lime, juice and zest
1/2 cup/125 ml light soy sauce
1/4 cup/50 ml creamed honey
2 garlic cloves, minced
12-16 long bamboo skewers, soaked in water
juice of 2 limes
salt and pepper to taste

Place salmon and vegetables into a large, flat dish. In a small bowl whisk together the lime juice and zest, soy sauce, honey, and garlic until honey is dissolved; pour over salmon and vegetables. Season with salt and pepper. Toss everything gently together, cover and refrigerate for 6 hours.

Preheat barbeque to medium-high and oil the grill. Alternate the marinated salmon and vegetables onto the soaked skewers.

In a small bowl, whisk together the lime juice and honey.

Place skewers on hot grill and cook 10 minutes, basting often with honey mixture, and turning once.

Serves 6.

Maple Pistachio Salmon

2 fresh salmon fillets, 8 oz/225 g each
1/2 cup/125 ml pure maple syrup
1/2 cup/125 ml shelled pistachios, chopped small

Lightly brush salmon with small amount of syrup to help pistachios stick. Top salmon with pistachios, place onto an oven-proof pan lined with parchment paper.

Pour remaining syrup over both salmon fillets; place into a 375°F – 400°F/190°C – 200°C oven and bake for approximately 10 minutes or until cooked through.

Remove and serve with mashed potatoes. Pour remaining syrup from pan over salmon and enjoy.

Serves 2.

Govern a great nation as you would cook
a small fish. Do not overdo it.

– Chinese Taoist philosopher Lao-Tzu

Poached Salmon

whole fresh salmon
1 onion, sliced
1 Tbsp/15 ml vinegar or fresh lemon juice
2 carrots, chopped
celery, chopped
herbs

4 egg yolks
1 Tbsp/15 ml tarragon vinegar
1 1/2 cup/375 ml olive oil
2 Tbsp/30 ml thick cream
1/2 cup/125 ml fresh cooked spinach (pass spinach through a sieve)
salt and pepper to taste

Wash salmon, pat dry, wrap and tie in a cheesecloth. Bring to a boil
enough water to cover the fish, plus sliced onion, vinegar or fresh lemon
juice, carrots, celery, herbs, and salt to taste. When the liquid has boiled
for a few minutes, reduce heat and simmer gently. Place fish in liquid
and cook 10 minutes per inch (2.5 cm) of thickness. When cooked, lift
from pan carefully and unwrap. Remove the skin and flake off brown
meat. Serve with green sauce (recipe below) and place on a large platter.
Garnish. One-half pound/225 g of dressed salmon serves one adult.

Green Sauce
In a mixing bowl small enough to be placed in a pan of water, mix egg
yolks, tarragon vinegar, salt, and pepper. Set the bowl in a pan of warm
water and heat on medium. Stirring constantly, add the oil, cream, and
spinach. As soon as the mixture becomes thick and smooth, spread
over the poached salmon. The salmon may then be served hot or cold
on a platter garnished with parsley and lemon wedges.

*(this recipe won a Gold Medal for Canada in competition with
17 other countries in Berne, Switzerland, 1954)*

Poached Salmon with Egg-Caper Sauce

4 lb/2 kg piece centre-cut
  salmon w/bone and skin
1 carrot, peeled and sliced
1 stalk celery, sliced
1 medium yellow onion, peeled
  and quartered
1 lemon, thinly sliced

2 bay leaves
6 black peppercorns
5 sprigs fresh dill
5 sprigs fresh parsley
2 cups/500 ml dry white wine
salt to taste

Egg-Caper Sauce:
1 1/2 Tbsp/22 ml butter
1 1/2 Tbsp/22 ml flour
1 cup/250 ml fish stock, warmed (see step 2)
1/2 cup/125 ml heavy cream
2 hard-boiled eggs, peeled and chopped
2 Tbsp/30 ml capers, rinsed and coarsely chopped
salt and pepper

Place carrots, celery, onions, lemon slices, bay leaves, and
peppercorns in a large, deep roasting pan. Rub salmon with salt,
then lay on top of vegetables. Add dill, parsley, white wine, and just
enough water to cover.

Place pan over two stove-top burners and bring to a simmer over
medium heat. Cook until salmon is pink, about 35 minutes, then
remove from heat. Let salmon rest in poaching liquid for 5 minutes,
then transfer to a work surface, peel skin from one side, and scrape
off dark flesh with a knife. Reserve poaching liquid to use in egg-
caper sauce or other recipes calling for fish stock.

Lift off top filet of salmon, transfer to a platter, then remove salmon
backbone and any other visible bones. Turn fish over, and peel skin

and scrape off dark flesh as in step 2, then transfer remaining filet to platter. Serve warm with egg-caper sauce.

Egg-Caper Sauce: Melt butter in a small, heavy saucepan over medium heat. Add flour and cook, whisking constantly, until mixture is bubbling, about 2 minutes (do not brown). Slowly whisk in fish stock and heavy cream. Bring to a simmer and cook for 30 seconds, then remove from heat and set aside to cool for 5 minutes. (Sauce will thicken as it rests.) Stir in eggs and capers. Season to taste with salt and pepper. Keep warm over low heat and serve with poached salmon. Makes 2 cups.

Serves 4 to 6.

All cats love fish but fear
to wet their paws.

–Chinese proverb

Salmon Frittata

1 cup/250 ml flaked cooked salmon
4 large eggs
2 Tbsp/30 ml sour or regular cream
1 Tbsp/15 ml cream cheese (optional)
1 Tbsp/15 ml olive oil
2 Tbsp/30 ml feta cheese
1/3 cup/75 ml roasted red pepper, chopped
3 Tbsp/45 ml scallions, both white and green parts, chopped
1 to 2 Tbsp/15 to 30 ml freshly grated parmesan cheese
2 tsp/10 ml water

Preheat the oven to 375°F – 400°F/190° C – 200°C.

Stir together the eggs, water, sour cream, and cream cheese, if using. Set aside. Put the olive oil into a shallow baking dish. Heat on the stove. Add the egg mixture. Sprinkle with the feta cheese, red pepper, salmon, and scallions. Bake for 15 to 25 minutes, or until the eggs are cooked through. Sprinkle with parmesan cheese and cook about 3 minutes longer, or until the cheese is melted, forming a glaze.

Serves 2.

Salmon with Salsa

2 fresh salmon fillets, 8 oz/225 g each
1/2 cup/125 ml dark rum
1/8 cup/25 ml brown sugar
1/4 cup/50 ml soy sauce

Citrus Salsa:
1/2 cup/125 m lemon segments
1/2 cup/125 ml lime segments
1/2 cup/125 ml orange segments
1/2 cup/125 ml grapefruit segments
1/8 cup/25 ml lemon zest
honey to taste

Preheat oven to 375°F – 400°F/190°C – 200°C.

Combine rum, sugar, and soy sauce over heat until dissolved. Cool.
Marinate salmon overnight.

Prepare citrus salsa by mixing all ingredients together; add honey to
taste.

Take salmon out of marinade and bake in baking dish for 10 to 15
minutes or until done. Do not overbake.

Serve salmon over a bed of rice topped with the fresh citrus salsa.

Serves 2.

Salmon Wellington

4 fresh salmon fillets,
   8 oz/225 g each
1/2 cup/125 ml shrimp, cooked
1/2 cup/125 ml butter
1 tsp/5 ml garlic, minced
8 sheets phyllo pastry

2 tsp/10 ml cream cheese
1/4 tsp/1 ml tarragon
1/4 tsp/1 ml basil
1/4 cup/50 ml mozzarella
   cheese, grated
melted butter, as needed

Preheat oven to 375°F – 400°F/190°C – 200°C.

Melt butter and add minced garlic.

Take 2 sheets of phyllo pastry; brush with garlic butter and fold in half to form a triangle 6" x 9"/15 x 23 cm. Repeat 3 more times and cover.

Place salmon on bottom of pastry. Brush salmon with garlic butter. Place shrimp, cheeses and spices in centre of salmon.

Fold pastry over, tuck in ends, and brush with butter. Place pastry on a greased cookie sheet. Brush top with butter. Cut 2 air vents into pastry.

Bake for approximately 30 minutes.

Serves 4.

Stuffed Salmon with Cucumber Dill Sauce

1 whole fresh salmon (3-4 lbs/1350 g-2 kg)
1 orange, sliced
1 lemon, sliced
1 cup/250 ml fresh dill, chopped

Stuff the whole salmon with orange and lemon slices, and half the chopped dill. Set aside 1 tsp/5 ml of the dill for the sauce and sprinkle the rest around the outside of the salmon. Double wrap in aluminum foil, making sure the seams are double folded, and place on hot barbeque grill. Turn occasionally. When the foil wrap puffs up, the salmon is done. Serve in sections.

Cucumber Dill Sauce:
6 oz/175 g container plain yogurt
1 medium cucumber, peeled and chopped
1 tsp/5 ml fresh dill
1 tsp/5 ml brown sugar
1/2 tsp/2 ml salt
1/4 tsp/1 ml pepper
1/2 tsp/2 ml Tabasco sauce

While the fish is cooking, combine sauce ingredients in a bowl. Serve with cooked salmon.

Serves 4 to 6.

Broiled Sardines and Pesto

20 fresh large sardines, scaled and gutted
2 cups/500 ml fresh basil leaves
2 garlic cloves, minced
2 Tbsp/30 ml pine nuts, toasted
1/2 cup/125 ml freshly grated parmesan cheese
2/3 cup/150 ml olive oil
salt and pepper

Garnish with:
fresh dill sprigs
lemon wedges
strips of lemon rind

Wash the sardines under cold running water and pat dry on paper towels. Arrange on a broiler pan.

To make the pesto, put the basil leaves, garlic, and pine nuts into a food processor and process until finely chopped. Transfer to a small bowl and stir in the parmesan cheese and olive oil. Season to taste with salt and pepper.

Spread a little of the pesto over one side of the sardines and place under a preheated hot broiler for 3 minutes. Turn the fish, spread with more pesto, and broil for another 3 minutes until the sardines are cooked.

Transfer the fish to serving plates, garnish with a few sprigs of fresh dill and lemon wedges. Serve immediately with extra pesto, garnished with strips of lemon rind.

Serves 4.

Scallops with Curried Leeks and Orange Sauce

1 lb/455 g fresh large sea scallops, washed and patted dry with
   paper towels
2 1/2 cups/625 ml orange juice
3 sprigs fresh thyme
4 Tbsp/60 ml unsalted butter, softened
2 large leeks, white part only, washed and julienned
3 Tbsp/45 ml curry powder
3 Tbsp/45 ml olive oil
salt and pepper to taste

In a saucepan set over high heat, bring the orange juice and thyme
to a boil. Cook until reduced to 1/2 cup/125 ml liquid, 8 to 10
minutes. Strain, return the sauce to the pan, and set aside.

In a sauté pan set over low heat, melt 2 Tbsp/30 ml of the butter.
Add the leeks and cook slowly, stirring frequently, for 3 minutes. Add
the curry powder and continue cooking until the leeks are tender,
about 5 minutes.

Heat the olive oil in a cast-iron or other heavy skillet over high heat.
Season the scallops with salt and pepper. When the oil is lightly
smoking, sear the scallops until golden brown on both sides, about 3
minutes total.

Reheat the reduced juice until it boils, remove from the heat, and
rapidly whisk in the remaining 2 Tbsp/30 ml of butter.

Mound the leeks in the centre of two warm plates. Arrange the
scallops on top of the leeks and top the scallops with the sauce.

Serves 2.

Scallops with Mangoes and Limes

2 lb/1 kg large fresh sea scallops
1 mango
1/4 cup/50 ml olive oil
1 lime, cut in 8 wedges
pepper to taste
juice and zest of a lime

Soak 8 wooden skewers in water for an hour. Cut the mango into chunks roughly the size of the scallops. Cut the desired shape on the mango skin and through to the pit. Then cut the chunk away from the pit. Don't remove the skin until after you separate the flesh from the pit. Combine the olive oil, pepper, and lime zest and juice in a small dish. Thread the mangoes and scallops equally on the 8 skewers. End with a wedge of lime on each skewer. Preheat barbeque to medium-high and grill, brushing with the marinade and turning as needed to keep the scallops from browning too heavily. Grill until the outside of the scallops is nicely browned and the inside is just cooked through. When eating, squeeze the lime wedge over the scallops and mangoes.

Serves 4.

Seafood Brochettes

4 large fresh sea scallops
4 raw peeled and deveined jumbo shrimp
4 white mushrooms
4 cherry tomatoes
4 baby corn (optional)
2 Tbsp/30 ml olive oil, for basting
flat-leaf parsley sprigs, to garnish
buttered rice, to serve

If using wooden skewers, soak them in water for 30 minutes before using to prevent burning. Preheat the grill to medium heat.

Meanwhile, thread scallops and shrimp and the vegetables alternately onto each skewer.

Put the kabobs on the grill and cook, turning frequently and basting occasionally with oil, for approximately 5 minutes until the vegetables are tender.

Remove the kabobs from the heat and transfer to individual serving plates. Garnish with parsley and serve with buttered rice.

Serves 2.

Balsamic Grilled Shark

Contrary to the rule of grilling fish 10 minutes per inch of thickness, shark needs only 7 to 8 minutes per inch of thickness. Overcooking makes shark tough.

4 fresh shark steaks, 8 oz/225 g each

Balsamic Marinade:
1/2 cup/125 ml olive oil
1/4 cup/50 ml balsamic vinegar
1 1/2 Tbsp/22 ml sugar
1 Tbsp/15 ml Worcestershire sauce
2 medium-size green onions, minced
1 tsp/5 ml dry mustard
1 garlic clove, minced
Tabasco sauce to taste
salt and pepper to taste

Combine the marinade ingredients and pour into a resealable plastic bag. Add the shark steaks, seal, and shake to coat them. Refrigerate for about 1 hour.

Preheat barbeque to medium-high.

Grill steaks until opaque, about 4 minutes per side, turning once and basting occasionally with the marinade. Do not overcook.

Also good with monkfish or swordfish.

Serves 4.

Grilled Shark with Green Peppercorns

Shark, when bought fresh, is wonderful lightly grilled or stewed. When buying, check that the colour is pale and creamy and with no aroma. You will instantly know when the shark is not fresh as it will smell of ammonia.

4 fresh shark steaks,
    8 oz/225 g each
1 Tbsp/15 ml green peppercorns,
preferably those in brine
3 garlic cloves, minced
pinch of saffron

juice and zest of 1/2 lemon
handful of fresh parsley,
    chopped
2/3 cup/150 ml olive oil

First make the dressing, which also acts as a marinade in this dish, by combining together the green peppercorns, garlic, parsley, saffron, lemon zest, and olive oil. Spoon over the shark so that it is covered well and leave in the fridge to marinate for at least 1-2 hours.

Pre-heat the grill or barbecue and place the shark steaks on or under the grill for 4 to 5 minutes on each side until just cooked through. Place them on a plate with a squeeze of lemon and the remaining marinade and accompany with a salad of sliced tomato, red onion, coriander, and lime juice.

Serves 4.

Louisiana Baked Shrimp

Serve these tasty baked shrimp with plenty of crusty bread to mop up the rich butter sauce.

1 lb/455 g large, raw peeled and deveined shrimp
1/4 cup/50 ml unsalted butter or margarine
1/4 cup/50 ml dry red wine
1 tsp/5 ml chili powder
1 tsp/5 ml freshly ground black pepper
1 tsp/5 ml minced garlic
2 tsp/10 ml Worcestershire sauce
1/4 tsp/1 ml salt
1/8 tsp/.5 ml ground red pepper
French or Italian bread

Place shrimp in a single layer in small, ungreased baking dish.

Combine butter and all ingredients except bread in a saucepan. Cook over medium heat, stirring constantly, until butter melts. Pour over shrimp. Bake, uncovered, at 400°F/200°C for 6 to 8 minutes or until shrimp turn pink. Serve with bread.

Serves 2.

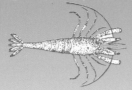

Shrimp Mignonette

24 raw jumbo shrimp, peeled and deveined
1/4 cup/50 ml butter
1 tsp/5 ml onion, finely chopped
1/4 tsp/1 ml crushed garlic
1/4 tsp/1 ml tarragon
1/2 tsp/2 ml chives, chopped
2 tsp/10 ml parsley, chopped
1/2 tsp/2 ml salt
1/2 tsp/2 ml freshly ground black pepper
1/4 tsp/1 ml paprika
2 Tbsp/30 ml dry sherry
3 Tbsp/45 ml dried bread crumbs
lemon wedges
fresh parsley

Melt butter in a skillet, add garlic, onion, tarragon, chives, pepper, salt, sherry, and shrimp. Cook 3 minutes. Add breadcrumbs, mixing well. Turn into a baking dish and arrange shrimp in neat rows or in a circular pattern. Sprinkle with paprika and half the parsley, and bake at 375°F – 400°F/190°C – 200°C for 15 minutes or until the breadcrumbs brown a little. Just before serving, sprinkle with remaining chopped parsley and arrange the lemon wedges and sprigs of parsley around the serving dish.

Serves 4.

Shrimp Roquefort

1 lb/455 g of large, raw, peeled and deveined shrimp
juice of 1 lime
1/4 cup/50 ml butter, melted
6 Tbsp/90 ml cream cheese
2 Tbsp/30 ml roquefort or other blue cheese
salt and pepper to taste

Place shrimps in a baking dish. Sprinkle with salt and pepper and the lime juice. Blend butter and both cheeses together and pour over shrimps. Cover with aluminum foil. Bake in a 375°F – 400°F/190°C – 200°C oven for approximately 8 minutes.

Serves 2.

Shrimp Sautéed in Butter

12 large, raw, peeled and deveined shrimp
1/2 cup/125 ml butter
3 shallots, chopped
6 fresh medium-sized mushrooms, thinly sliced
1 tomato, diced
1/4 cup/50 ml white wine
1 garlic clove, minced
fresh parsley, chopped

Sauté shrimps in butter. While cooking, add all other ingredients. Serve on a bed of rice.

Serves 2.

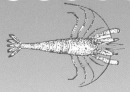

Tequila Shrimp

2 lb/1 kg large, raw, peeled and deveined fresh shrimp
1/4 cup/50 ml olive oil
1/4 cup/50 ml tequila
1/4 cup/50 ml fresh lime juice
2 garlic cloves, crushed
1 tsp/5 ml dried crushed red pepper
2 Tbsp/30 ml red wine vinegar
1/2 tsp/2 ml salt
1 medium-size sweet red pepper, cut into thin strips
1 medium-size green pepper, cut into thin strips
1 medium-size red onion, cut into eighths

Place shrimp in an ungreased large baking dish. Set aside.

Combine olive oil and all ingredients except peppers and onion in a jar. Cover tightly, and shake to mix. Pour over shrimp. Place sweet red pepper, green pepper, and onion on top of shrimp. Cover and marinate in refrigerator 1 hour.

Remove shrimp and vegetables from marinade, reserving marinade. Set shrimp and vegetables aside. Bring marinade to a boil in a small saucepan; set aside.

Thread shrimp evenly onto metal skewers. Grill shrimp, covered, over medium coals (300F/150°C to 350°F/180°C) 2 minutes on each side, basting occasionally with cooked marinade. Set aside, and keep warm.

Cook vegetables in any remaining marinade in a large skillet over medium-high heat, stirring constantly, until tender. Serve shrimp with vegetables.

Serves 4.

Thai Coconut Curry Shrimp

2 lb/1 kg of large, raw, peeled
  and deveined shrimp
1 Tbsp/15 ml thai green curry
  paste
Thai fish sauce (*nam pla*)
1 can coconut milk

chili garlic sauce
1 can tomatoes, diced
green onions, chopped
fresh cilantro, chopped
roasted peanuts or cashews

In a saucepan, heat a can of coconut milk, whisk in a tablespoon/15 ml (or more if you want it hotter) of the Thai green curry paste. Add a bit of the chili garlic sauce to taste, a couple shakes of Thai fish sauce, and the can of tomatoes. Simmer a few minutes. Stir in shrimp. Cook only till they turn pink, being careful not to overcook. Serve over basmati or jasmine rice. Sprinkle on cilantro, nuts, and green onions. This recipe is also great with scallops or a combination of shrimp and scallops. If too hot, stir in some plain yogurt.

Try your local Asian market to find green curry, fish sauce, and coconut milk.

Serves 4.

Baked Sole Dijon

1 lb/455 g fresh sole fillets
1 tsp/5 ml melted butter
1/2 cup/125 ml mayonnaise
1/4 cup/50 ml Dijon mustard
2 Tbsp/30 ml chives, chopped

Place sole in a lightly buttered baking dish. Combine remaining ingredients in a small bowl; spread evenly over fish fillets. Bake at 375°F – 400°F/190°C – 200°C for approximately 10 minutes, or until fish flakes easily with a fork.

Serves 2.

That fish will soon be caught that nibbles at every bait.

–Thomas Fuller, *Gnomologia*

Delightful Sole Meunière

2 lb/1 kg fresh sole fillets
1 cup/250 ml milk
3/4 cup/175 ml flour
2 Tbsp/30 ml butter
1–2 Tbsp/15–30 ml sunflower oil
2 Tbsp/30 ml fresh parsley, chopped
salt and pepper to taste
lemon wedges, to garnish

Pour the milk into a large, shallow dish. Spread the flour out on a large, flat plate and season to taste with salt and pepper.

Dip the sole in the milk and then in the flour, turning to coat. Shake off any excess.

Melt the butter with the oil in a large, heavy-bottom skillet over low heat, add the fish fillets, and cook for 2–3 minutes on each side until lightly browned. Sprinkle with the parsley and serve at once, garnished with lemon wedges.

Serves 4.

Baked Swordfish with Rosemary and Garlic

2 fresh swordfish steaks, 8 oz/225 g each
1/4 cup/50 ml olive oil
2 garlic cloves, crushed to a paste
handful of rosemary branches
lemon juice
sea salt

Preheat your oven to 375°F – 400°F/190°C – 200°C.

Place the swordfish steaks in a roasting dish.

In a small saucepan, gently warm the oil, garlic, and rosemary for approximately 3-4 minutes.

Pour the oil over the swordfish and place in the oven for 8-10 minutes. Then just add a squeeze of lemon, a sprinkling of sea salt and serve.

Serves 2.

Pan-Roasted Swordfish Steaks with Peppercorn Butter

4 fresh swordfish steaks, 8 oz/225 g each
3 Tbsp/45 ml olive oil
1/4 cup/50 ml butter, room temperature
2 tsp/10 ml fresh parsley, chopped
1 garlic clove, minced
1/2 tsp/2 ml ground mixed peppercorns, plus more for sprinkling
1/2 tsp/2 ml lemon zest
salt to taste

Preheat oven to 375°F - 400°F/190°C - 200°C. Mash butter, parsley, garlic, 1/2 tsp/2 ml peppercorns, and lemon zest in small bowl. Season to taste with salt.

In heavy large ovenproof skillet, heat oil over medium-high heat. Sprinkle swordfish with salt and ground peppercorns. Add swordfish to skillet. Cook until browned, about 3 minutes. Turn swordfish over and transfer to oven. Roast until just cooked through, about 5-7 minutes longer. Transfer swordfish to plates. Add seasoned butter to same skillet. Cook over medium-high heat, scraping up browned bits, until melted and bubbling. Pour butter sauce over swordfish and serve.

Serves 4

Tilapia in White Wine Sauce

4 fresh tilapia fillets, 8 oz/225 g each
1 1/2 cup/375 ml dry vermouth
8 egg yolks
2 Tbsp/30 ml shallot, chopped
2 Tbsp/30 ml parsley, chopped
1 1/4 cup/300 ml butter pieces
2 Tbsp/30 ml heavy cream
salt and pepper to taste

In a skillet, bring the vermouth, shallot, and parsley to a boil. Lower the heat and simmer 10 minutes. Add the tilapia and poach gently until it flakes easily with a fork. There should be enough wine to cover the fillets. Add more wine if necessary. Move the fillets to a flat ovenproof baking dish, season with salt and pepper, and keep warm. Boil the liquid until it is reduced to 1/2 cup/125 ml. In the top of a double boiler, mix the cooking liquid, butter, and egg yolks. Mix the sauce until it thickens. Add the heavy cream and pour the sauce over the fillets. Place under a hot broiler for a few seconds to glaze the top. Serve at once.

Serves 4.

◄LAPOINTE►

Almond Trout

2 fresh whole rainbow trout, 8 oz/225 g each, cleaned
flour, to coat
1/4 cup/50 ml butter
1/4 cup/50 ml flaked almonds
2 Tbsp/30 ml lemon juice
1 Tbsp/15 ml fresh parsley, finely chopped
salt and pepper

Coat the fish with the flour. Heat half the butter in a large frying pan and add the fish. Cook on medium-high heat for 7 minutes on each side, or until golden brown and cooked through. Remove and place on heated plates. Cover with foil.

Heat the remaining butter, add the flaked almonds, and stir until the almonds are light golden brown. Add the lemon juice, parsley, and some salt and pepper. Stir until the sauce is heated through. Pour over the trout and serve.

Serves 2.

Fish got to swim, birds got to fly.

–Oscar Hammerstein song, "Can't Help Lovin' Dat Man,"

Bacon-Wrapped Trout

4 fresh whole trout, cleaned
4 lean bacon slices
1/4 cup/50 ml flour
2 Tbsp/30 ml olive oil
salt and pepper
corn salad, to serve
lemon juice

Garnish:
fresh parsley sprigs
lemon wedges

Preheat the barbecue to medium-high. Rinse the trout inside and out under cold running water and pat dry with paper towels.

Spread the flour out on a large, flat plate and season to taste with salt and pepper. Gently roll each trout in the seasoned flour until well coated, then shake off any excess. Beginning just below the head, wrap a bacon slice in a spiral along the length of each fish.

Brush the trout with oil and cook over medium-high heat for 5–8 minutes on each side. Transfer to 4 large serving plates and serve with a squeeze of lemon. Garnish with parsley sprigs and lemon wedges.

Serves 4.

Grilled Tuna with Eggplant and Olives

2 fresh tuna steaks, 8 oz/225 g each
1 eggplant
1 garlic clove
1 Tbsp/15 ml black pitted olives
2/3 cup/150 ml olive oil
handful of coriander, chopped
lemon juice

Roast the eggplant whole in a low oven for 1–2 hours until soft. It will look almost deflated. Allow to cool and then peel.

Place the eggplant flesh in a food processor with the garlic and olives and pulse to a paste. Slowly drizzle in enough olive oil to form a smooth emulsion and then add the coriander.

To cook the tuna, brush it with olive oil and season and place on a preheated grill pan. Allow 2 to 4 minutes each side then remove and place on a plate. Top with the eggplant and a squeeze of lemon juice.

Serves 2.

Grilled Tuna with Wasabi Butter

4 fresh tuna steaks, 8 oz/225 g each
1/4 cup/50 ml olive oil
juice of 1 lemon
2 Tbsp/30 ml peeled fresh ginger, crushed
6 Tbsp/90 ml unsalted butter, softened
1/4 cup/50 ml wasabi (powdered horseradish)
salt and pepper to taste

Preheat barbeque or grill to medium-high heat.

Lay the tuna steaks in a large, shallow pan in one layer. Combine the olive oil, lemon juice, and ginger in a small bowl and pour over the fish. Let sit for 20 to 30 minutes. Turn the fish once in the marinade. Mix the butter and wasabi together into a thick paste. Set aside.

Season the steaks lightly with salt and pepper and grill them for about 2 to 4 minutes per side. Tuna dries out quickly so keep it moist with the marinade while cooking. Transfer the steaks to a platter and top each one with a teaspoon or tablespoon of the wasabi butter. Serve at once.

Serves 4.

Pan-fried
Tuna/Halibut/Swordfish

4 tuna, halibut or swordfish steaks, 8 oz/225 g each
8 shiitake or 6 medium-size portobello mushrooms, stems removed
10 ripe plum tomatoes
1 large or 2 small jalapeño peppers (optional)
3 Tbsp/45 ml olive oil
1/2 cup/125 ml pitted black olives, chopped
olive oil
salt and pepper to taste

For sauce, slice mushrooms into 1/4-inch thick strips. Core tomatoes, then slice in half. Squeeze out all juice and seeds and discard. Coarsely chop tomatoes. They should measure about 4 cups/1 L. Seed and finely chop jalapeño, if using. It should measure about 2 Tbsp/30 ml.

Heat oil in a large frying pan set over medium-high heat. When hot, add mushrooms. Then sprinkle with salt. Stir-fry just until lightly browned, about 5 minutes. Stir in tomatoes, jalapeño, and chopped olives. Cook over medium-high heat, uncovered, and stirring often (especially near end of cooking), until most of liquid is evaporated and sauce is thick. This will take about 15 minutes. Add more salt, if needed. Use sauce right away or refrigerate, covered, for up to 2 days. Reheat over low heat or on medium power in microwave, stirring often.

To sear tuna, lightly coat a frying pan with oil. Place over medium-high heat. Lightly salt tuna and liberally sprinkle with pepper. Place in hot pan. Sear from 2 to 4 minutes per side. (Two minutes per side will leave it very rare.) Place on warm dinner plates and top with sauce.

Serves 4.

INDEX